The Apostolic Faith Mission Complex History

Jaison Ndlovu

Published by Jaison Ndlovu, 2024.

While every precaution has been taken in the preparation of this book, the publisher assumes no responsibility for errors or omissions, or for damages resulting from the use of the information contained herein.

THE APOSTOLIC FAITH MISSION COMPLEX HISTORY

First edition. August 10, 2024.

ISBN: 979-8227560476

Written by Jaison Ndlovu.

Table of Contents

Introduction 1

CHAPTER one...4

CHAPTER two 13

CHAPTER three 22

CHAPTER four..30

CHAPTER five...37

CHAPTER six...47

CHAPTER seven 55

CHAPTER eight 61

CHAPTER Nine 71

CHAPTER ten 81

To my daughter, Lomalinda Grannie Ndhlovu, whose inspiring idea ignited this journey. To my sons Logic Amos, Eureka Eulogy, Russell Hillary and Elisha Heritage, not forgeting their sister, Misery, whose unwavering support and material assistance fueled its progression. To my spouse, Susan Ndlovu (nee Mahogo), whose genuine interest provided constant motivation. And to my dear mother, Resiya Magundwane, (nee Chikwinya), whose prayers guided every word written. To my grandchildren who I have always wanted to know and tell when I am gone. Last but not least, all my relatives. This book is a testament to the love, encouragement, and unity that has always surrounded me.

Introduction

In this comprehensive discussion, we will delve into the rich history of the Apostolic Faith Mission (AFM) in Zimbabwe, beginning with the humble origins of my village assembly. We will explore how this local assembly connects with the broader denomination, tracing the roots of the AFM and its evolution over time.

Our examination will also reveal the intricate web of connections between the AFM and its various offshoots, which have emerged throughout its century-plus long history. We will analyze the factors that have contributed to the formation of these offshoots, including theological differences, leadership disputes, and cultural influences.

Furthermore, we will investigate the interconnectedness of the Church with its origins, exploring how the AFM's early beginnings have shaped its current identity and practices. This will involve examining the role of key figures, such as John G. Lake and Thomas Hezmalhalch, who played a significant part in shaping the AFM's theology and mission.

As we navigate the complex history of the AFM, we will also consider the lessons that can be learned from its experiences. If our leaders were to take heed of these lessons, what would be the best way forward for the denomination? How can the AFM build upon its strengths while addressing its weaknesses and divisions?

Through this discussion, we aim to gain a deeper understanding of the AFM's history, its connections with other churches and denominations, and its potential for growth and unity in the future. By exploring the complexities of the AFM's past, we hope to uncover valuable insights that can inform its path forward.

While it's true that research often builds upon existing knowledge, We're constrained to rely solely on the Bible as our primary source, due to the nature of this project. This is because some of the information is derived from readily available sources, including online materials and hardcopy resources that can be easily accessed without extensive effort. Additionally, a portion of the narrative comes from trustworthy oral sources, which have been shared through personal accounts and testimonies. By drawing from these sources, we aim to present a comprehensive and accurate account, grounded in biblical truth and supplemented by reliable oral traditions.

Although our primary focus in this narrative will be on the Apostolic Faith Mission (AFM) in Zimbabwe, it is essential to acknowledge the inextricable link between the Zimbabwean chapter and its South African counterpart. The history of the "whites only" AFM of South Africa, which operated within Zimbabwe's borders, will not be explored in exhaustive detail, as it is not crucial to our main discussion. However, we will touch on relevant aspects of its history to provide context.

Our narrative will unfold chronologically, tracing key events and milestones in the history of AFM in Zimbabwe. When a significant theme or issue arises, we will delve into it thoroughly, exploring its implications and impact, before returning to the chronological sequence of events. This approach will enable us to grasp the complexities and nuances of the AFM's journey in Zimbabwe, while also highlighting the critical intersections with its South African roots.

And the story in general is that my grandfather, Jenias Mufambi Chikwinya's, passing in 1972 sparked a quest to uncover the rich history of the Apostolic Faith Mission (AFM) in Zimbabwe. Through family accounts and research, I've pieced together a narrative that spans generations, exploring the church's development, challenges, and triumphs.

The AFM's roots trace back to Charles Fox Parham and the Azusa Street Revival, shaping the global Pentecostal movement. John Graham Lake founded the AFM in South Africa in 1908, emphasizing divine healing, evangelism, and the Pentecostal experience. The church grew rapidly, but faced splits and divisions, including Lake's departure in 1913.

In Zimbabwe, the AFM was introduced by immigrant workers in 1908 and gained recognition in 1943. Missionaries like Dugmore and Manamela played key roles in spreading the Pentecostal message around 1915. Pieter Luttig's ministry in Kadoma from 1918 thrived, despite challenges and controversies. Enoch Gwanzura, a pivotal figure, helped the church gain recognition and became a self-appointed head minister. His legacy continued through his family.

The AFM in Zimbabwe underwent a significant transformation in 1983, marking a new era of autonomy and self-determination. Langton Kupara assumed leadership, symbolizing the transition from foreign to local stewardship. However, the delayed transition raises questions about loyalty, segregation, and empowerment.

The AFM's history has been rewritten to prioritize certain narratives and agendas, marginalizing several pioneers and elders. This biased approach distorts the church's true heritage and undermines its integrity. The AFM has experienced numerous breakaways, including those led by Florence Crawford, Morgan Sengwayo, Engenas Lekganyane, Samuel Moyo, and Elijah Mugodhi. Despite these challenges, the AFM remains a significant player in the Pentecostal movement.

Through my research, I aim to honor the contributions of local leaders like my grandfather and uncover the rich history of the AFM in Zimbabwe. By exploring the church's development, challenges, and triumphs, I hope to provide a more comprehensive understanding of the AFM's role in shaping Zimbabwe's religious landscape.

CHAPTER one

From Kadoma to Zhombe: Unraveling the Complex History of the Local Church

In 1972, at the tender age of twelve, my world was forever changed when my beloved maternal grandfather, Jenias Mufambi Chikwinya, passed away. Little did I know that his departure would leave a void in my life, a void that would grow into an insatiable hunger to uncover the rich history of the Apostolic Faith Mission of South Africa's Zimbabwe mission field.

As I grew older, I yearned to ask him about the stories, the struggles, and the triumphs of our ancestors, but alas, he was gone.

Born in 1910 in Gutu, my grandfather, a devoted minister of religion, lived a remarkable life in both Chiundura Tribal Trust Land and Nyakapupu Purchase Area, Guruve, then called Sipolilo. Despite passing away at 62, he appeared to me, as a primary school student, to be one of the oldest individuals I had ever seen. Now, as I write this narrative at the age of 64, I am two years older than he was at the time of his passing. Yet, I marvel at how much younger I appear compared to how I perceived him in my youth.

My grandfather dedicated over 35 years of his life to serving as a native pastor or evangelist, as black pastors were classified then. Although he spent his final years as a sidelined evangelist due to lacking the necessary qualifications for Kasupe Bible College in Zambia, his commitment to his faith remained unwavering. Unfortunately, during that era, the governments of South Africa and Southern Rhodesia did not recognize black individuals as legitimate pastors, viewing them instead as mere adherents. This discriminatory norm led John G. Lake to compromise, ensuring the Church's continued presence in these regions.

His eldest son, Naphtali Mufambi, born 1932, and my mother, Resiya Chikwinya, born 1934, were my only links to the past. Though their memories were sketchy, their words were gold dust to me. I pieced together their stories, and with each passing day, a vivid tapestry of our church history emerged.

This narrative also incorporates contributions from my father, Katazo Amos Magundwane, who embraced the faith after the passing of his first wife, during the time he courted my mother. My father, Katazo, was a valuable source of information about the later years of the Apostolic Faith Mission (AFM) of South Africa in Zimbabwe, specifically the period after 1950.

In crafting this narrative, I have drawn upon the collective knowledge and experiences shared by my mother and uncle, which were passed down to them from their father, my maternal grandfather, Jenias Mufambi Chikwinya. Their contributions have provided invaluable insights into the history of the Apostolic Faith Mission (AFM) in Zimbabwe. While I won't directly quote their statements or attribute specific comments to individuals, I have woven their accounts into my own narrative, supported by my own research and verification.

My family's knowledge primarily concerns the church's development within Zimbabwe, while their understanding of the church's history outside the country is based on information shared by missionaries and migrant workers. I have supplemented this with my own research to provide a comprehensive narrative.

Notably, there were other local religious ministers and evangelists, like Jenias Mufambi Chikwinya, who played significant roles in the AFM's growth, but remain undocumented in local records. Although some reports by white missionaries may have portrayed black evangelists in a negative light, and certain local Zimbabweans may have overlooked the contributions of colonial-era evangelists, I aim to acknowledge and honor their efforts in this narrative.

While I am unable to cite specific documents from the AFM of South Africa library due to lack of authorization, I assure readers that my account can be verified by visiting the library. I invite anyone interested in confirming the accuracy of my narrative to explore the library's resources and discover the rich history of the AFM in Southern Africa.

This research has been a bittersweet journey for me. On one hand, I'm grateful to have uncovered the rich history of the Apostolic Faith Mission (AFM) through reliable sources and personal experiences, having been born in 1960 and remained a loyal member ever since. On the other hand, I'm disheartened to witness the declining spiritual standards within the church. While educational, institutional, and numerical growth continue to soar, the fervor and passion of the past seem to be waning.

This phenomenon is not unique to the AFM, as the Azusa Revival of the early 20th century was similarly named because it marked a resurgence of spiritual practices that had dwindled since the Apostolic era. This historical context brings me some comfort, knowing that the Holy Spirit's wonderful works have faced similar challenges before. However, I'm not complacent and instead pray fervently for another revival to sweep through the church, restoring its former glory and reigniting the passion of its members. I yearn for a spiritual awakening that will revitalize the AFM, and I believe that with God's help, it can happen sooner rather than later.

Just as a fire requires constant fuel to maintain its intensity, the spiritual fervor and momentum of the early Apostolic Faith Mission (AFM) leaders, including Thomas Hezmalhalch and John Graham Lake, seemed to wane over time. Reviving the fire with different "wood" or approaches can alter its temperature and impact, often resulting in a weaker flame.

In contrast to the conventional practice of serving the best wine first and the inferior quality last, as seen at the wedding in Cana (John 2:9-10), the spiritual life is meant to be a journey of increasing intensity and passion, not dwindling embers. Just as the master of ceremonies was surprised by the superior quality of the wine miraculously provided by Jesus, surpassing the initial serving, so too should our spiritual fire burn brighter with time. This is echoed in Haggai 2:9, which declares that the glory of the latter house will exceed that of the former, signifying a progression towards greater spiritual depth and richness.

As the Apostle Paul cautioned, "Do not quench the Spirit" (1 Thessalonians 5:19-20). While God faithfully works to elevate His standard from glory to glory, human tendencies and institutional barriers can stifle the Spirit's movement. The church's constitution, often influenced by secular systems, can play a significant role in quenching the Spirit. Other factors, such as complacency, tradition, and power struggles, can also hinder the momentum of the Lord's work within the church. In subsequent narratives, we will explore the effects of these "spirit-quenching" elements and their impact on the AFM's trajectory.

Today, I proudly present this testament to my grandfather's legacy, a tribute to the man who ignited a fire within me to uncover our glorious spiritual past.

Before delving into my grandfather's account of the Apostolic Faith Mission of South Africa's Zimbabwean mission, now known as AFM in Zimbabwe, I would like to provide some context by discussing the establishment of our local church assembly, one of the oldest in the area. Then, I will trace its roots back in time, providing a historical foundation for the narrative that follows.

The roots of the Apostolic Faith Mission of South Africa (AFM) in Bharamasvesve, Zhombe date back to the 1940s. It was during this period that Johan Gwanzura, affectionately known as "Chihari," spent time near Theta Mine in Zhombe, Kwekwe District. It was there that he baptized Adfar James, who would go on to become the pioneering elder and evangelist in both Zhombe and Gokwe, laying the groundwork for the AFM's presence in the region.

Concurrently, a pivotal encounter took place in Sehosana, North Western Zhombe, when Mrs. Smoke, a member of the Apostolic Faith Mission (AFM) in Kadoma, visited her brother, Mlunjwa Dube. Her husband was employed at Gatooma Text Tiles in Martin Spur, just outside Kadoma. Mrs. Smoke, having been converted, shared the gospel with her brother and his family, leading to their conversion and the establishment of an AFM branch in Sehosana, Zhombe. Upon her return to Kadoma, Mrs. Smoke reported the new group of converts to the church leaders, who subsequently dispatched Deacon Adfar James to lead the fledgling church in Zhombe. Notably, Deacon James later married Mlunjwa Dube's eldest daughter, further solidifying the connection between the two families and the AFM community.

Deacon Adfar James's leadership was swiftly recognized, and he was ordained as an elder in a short span. He then had the privilege of baptizing the converts from Zhombe, including the esteemed Mlunjwa, Mudavanhu, Ntini, and Bafana Virima families, in the sacred waters of the Fafi River.

Before proceeding, I'd like to take a moment to explain the significant event of James Adfar baptizing the first converts in Zhombe, and the reasoning behind the Apostolic Faith Mission's (AFM) practice of triune baptism by immersion. This clarification will provide valuable context for understanding the church's beliefs and practices.

John G. Lake and his team delved into the Greek terminology of Matthew 28:19, where three action words are translated as "of" in English. Jesus taught that converts should be triunely baptized in the name "of" the Father, "of" the Son, and "of" the Holy Spirit. This verse contains three action verbs, leading to various interpretations.

I repeat, including the Greek verbs:

John G. Lake and his team explored the nuances of Matthew 28:19, where the Greek words "εἰς τὸ ὄνομα" (eis to onoma), meaning "into the name," are translated as "of" in English. Jesus instructed that converts should be baptized triunely εἰς τὸ ὄνομα (into the name) of the Father, εἰς τὸ ὄνομα of the Son, and εἰς τὸ ὄνομα of the Holy Spirit. This verse contains three action verbs: βαπτίζω (baptizō), meaning "to immerse" or "to submerge"; πορεύω (poreuō), meaning "to go" or "to proceed"; and μαθητεύω (mathēteuō), meaning "to disciple" or "to instruct." These verbs lead to various interpretations.

Some argue that baptism symbolizes death and resurrection (Romans 6:3, Colossians 2:12), questioning whether converts should die and resurrect εἰς τὸ ὄνομα (into the name) of the Father, then repeat the process εἰς τὸ ὄνομα of Jesus Christ and the Holy Spirit. While this perspective is valid according to Paul's teaching and the book of Acts (Acts 2:38, 8:12, 16), the Pentecostal revival brought a deeper understanding of the significance of triune baptism, emphasizing the believer's identification with the Father, the Son, and the Holy Spirit.

In Colossians 2:12 Paul again says: "having been buried with him in baptism, wherein ye were also raised with him through faith in the working of God, who raised him from the dead."

Baptism is the grave of the old man, and the birth of the new. As he sinks beneath the baptismal waters, the believer buries there all his corrupt affections and past sins; as he emerges thence, he rises regenerate, quickened to new hopes and new life."

In today's era, people may not be holier than the ancient church, but they have a better understanding of scriptures, fulfilling Daniel's prophecy that knowledge shall abound and scriptures will be understood better in the last days. The Bible doesn't specify who baptized Paul, possibly Ananias (Acts

22:16), which was more about washing away sins, similar to ancient Jewish beliefs. Paul himself taught that the ancient Israelites were baptized unto Moses (1 Corinthians 10:1-4).

Baptism holds a greater meaning than just dying and arising with Christ. The people mentioned in 1 Corinthians 15:29 seemed to understand baptism's significance, and Paul didn't rebuke their idea but used it to support his teaching on the resurrection of the dead. John the Baptist baptized with water, teaching that someone would come after him, baptizing with the Spirit and fire (Acts 1:5, 11:16), unrelated to dying and resurrection.

The converts baptized by John were rebaptized in water (Acts 19:3-5). It's unclear if those baptized before the Great Commission were rebaptized. Jesus' baptism (John 3:22-23, 4:1-2) and the baptism in Matthew 20:22-23 didn't involve water burial and resurrection. The Apostolic Faith Mission of South Africa advocates triune baptism by immersion, considering the three action verbs in Matthew 28:19.

In a broader perspective, the Israelites were baptized three times: at the Red Sea as a nation, in the river Jordan by John for repentance, and finally in the baptism ordered by Christ. This doesn't mean they died and rose three times, showing that baptism is a mystery beyond human understanding, not fully enclosed in Paul's teaching.

Now, back to Zhombe Assembly history: In the early 1950s, Mlunjwa Dube relocated to Bharamasvesve, where he was appointed Kraal Head (Village Head) under Headman Gwesela Kuva Ndebele. This marked the beginning of a new chapter for Mlunjwa and his family, who soon became integral to the community. His son, Shadreck Mlunjwa, married into the Mudavanhu family, while his daughters married into the Virima and Gwanzura families, respectively. Isaiah Virima, son of Bafanios Virima, and Tadius Gwanzura, an adopted son of Johan Gwanzura, became part of the extended family. Notably, Tadius had recently arrived from Njelele, near Gokwe, where he had settled after Adfar James' relocation from Theta Mine. As the Mlunjwa, Virima, and Gwanzura families put down roots in Bharamasvesve, the Mudavanhu family established themselves in Mvuramachena, northwest of Bharamasvesve, further solidifying the connections between these families and their place in the community.

By the early 1960s, Shadreck Mlunjwa, Tadius Gwanzura, and Isaiah Virima had all risen to leadership positions as Deacons within the church. Isaiah Virima would later assume the role of second elder in Zhombe, succeeding Adfar James. This period also saw the arrival of Mukombe from Sengezi, Zhombe, who had previously been converted in Kadoma. Mukombe joined the thriving Bharamasvesve church, further enriching the community with his presence and spiritual journey. As the church continued to grow and mature, these leaders played a vital role in shaping its development and fostering a spirit of unity and faith among its members.

The church's reach extended from Bharamasvesve to neighboring areas, including Somalala, Somthanyelo, Kasawi, and the now Bee Mine area, as well as parts of Samambwa east. Meanwhile, Elder Adfar James, affectionately known as "Adfari," pioneered the first church in Gokwe, near Gokwe Centre, in addition to the existing Bharamasvesve church. Adfari courageously evangelized areas surrounding and beyond Gokwe Centre. By the 1970s, the Zhombe church had grown to over fifty members, including children. The author's parents, Deacon Katazo Amos Magundwane and Deaconess Resiya Magundwane (née Chikwinya), were now at the Bharamasvesve Assembly, having relocated from Somalala in Zhombe East.

Concurrently, the Gokwe church was also expanding, with new members joining from the Kwekwe and Kadoma/Sanyati areas. By this time, Ngwenya, the third elder in Zhombe, initially resided in the Somapane area before relocating to Mhondoro.

Despite being a man who finds contentment in simplicity and lives modestly, just above the poverty line, I often find myself dreaming of having the means to build a memorial church in Bharamasvesve, a village that holds significant historical importance as the birthplace of the Apostolic Faith Mission (AFM) in Zhombe and Gokwe. However, during my visit in 2022, I was disheartened to discover that not a single soul in the village remained a member of the AFM.

The majority, including my own family, had relocated to other areas, leaving behind a community devoid of pastoral care and spiritual guidance.

As a result, many have turned to other churches or, worse still, fallen prey to cults. This reality weighs heavily on my heart, and I cry out to God for intervention. The village that once nurtured the roots of the AFM now lies spiritually barren, a testament to the neglect and abandonment of its people. Oh, that I had the resources to erect a beacon of hope, a memorial church that would revitalize the faith and restore the spiritual heritage of Bharamasvesve! May God stir the hearts of His people to revive this forgotten village and reignite the flame of His presence.

The Zhombe church, with various sub-assemblies around Zhombe (excluding the defunct Bharamasvesve), operated as a sub-assembly itself under the Kwekwe Assembly, led by Rev. Salatiel Gwanzura, son of Samson Gwanzura, one of the famous Gwanzura brothers, until 1995. In that year, Pastor Joseph Gibson Kaledza was appointed as its first autonomous pastor, marking a significant milestone in the church's history.

Following Pastor Kaledza's tenure, the church was led by a succession of pastors, including Onias Ngwenya, John Maphosa, Salatiel Gayihayi, Sifelani Tsikira, Mhangara, and Chateya. However, during Pastor Chateya's leadership, the church experienced a division, resulting in the formation of two separate entities: the AFM of Zimbabwe, led by Pastor Chateya, and the AFM in Zimbabwe, led by Pastor Samuel Chitekete. In 2020, Pastor Clarence Mafarikwa succeeded Pastor Chitekete as the leader of the AFM in Zimbabwe, while Pastor Chateya continued to head the AFM of Zimbabwe. Prior to the split, the church was known as the Apostolic Faith Mission in Zimbabwe, abbreviated as AFM in Zimbabwe. The division led to the formation of an offshoot, led by Pastor Chateya, which adopted the name Apostolic Faith Mission of Zimbabwe, whereas the remaining faction retained the original name, Apostolic Faith Mission in Zimbabwe.

The division that occurred was not isolated to Zhombe alone, but rather a nationwide phenomenon that affected the entire organization. The split was a national division, impacting various regions and branches of the Apostolic

Faith Mission in Zimbabwe, and not limited to the local assembly in Zhombe. This suggests that the underlying issues and factors contributing to the division were more widespread and complex, affecting the broader organization beyond a single location.

This brief history outlines the origins of the Church's local assembly. And so, the church's roots in Gokwe district can be traced back to Sehosana, near Fafi, and later took hold in Bharamasvesve village, Zhombe, from which it expanded to become a vibrant presence throughout much of the district.

Here, the Zhombe assembly has its origins approximately 25 years after the church first established itself in Zimbabwe (then known as Southern Rhodesia) and roughly 33 years after the founding of the original Apostolic Faith Mission of South Africa on May 25, 1908. This places the assembly's beginnings in the context of a broader historical narrative, highlighting its connection to the larger Apostolic Faith Mission movement.

To gain a deeper understanding, we must delve further back in time, beyond 1908, and explore the historical context that gave rise to the Apostolic Faith Mission as a whole, ultimately leading to the establishment of its South African chapter. This requires examining the roots and early development of the Apostolic Faith Mission, tracing its evolution and key events that shaped its growth, and understanding the factors that contributed to the formation of its South African branch.

The designation "of South Africa" in the church's original name, Apostolic Faith Mission of South Africa, implies that the Apostolic Faith Mission was already present in other locations beyond South Africa. This suggests that the movement had a broader international presence before the South African chapter was established, and that the name was meant to distinguish the South African branch from existing ones elsewhere.

CHAPTER two

From Azusa to Africa: Unpacking the Historical Threads of the AFM of South Africa

The Church's history begins with the background of its founder, John Graham Lake, a remarkable figure in the history of Christian healing and ministry. Born on March 18, 1870, in Ontario, Canada, Lake dedicated his life to serving God and spreading the message of salvation and divine healing. His impact on the Christian faith and the lives of countless individuals is profound and continues to be felt to this day.

Lake felt a calling to ministry from a young age and pursued theological studies to prepare himself for his life's work. He eventually became a powerful preacher and evangelist, traveling extensively to share the gospel and pray for the sick. It was during his ministry travels that Lake witnessed numerous miracles of healing and deliverance, which became a hallmark of his work.

One of Lake's most significant contributions to Christian ministry was his emphasis on divine healing. He believed in the power of prayer and faith to bring about physical, emotional, and spiritual healing. Lake often spoke about the importance of faith in receiving healing and encouraged believers to trust in God's promises for their well-being.

In 1908, Lake founded the Apostolic Faith Mission in South Africa, where he continued his ministry of preaching, healing, and deliverance. The mission quickly grew in popularity and became a center for supernatural manifestations and revival. People from all walks of life came to the mission seeking healing and spiritual renewal, and many reported miraculous healings and transformations.

Lake's ministry was marked by a deep sense of compassion and love for others. He dedicated himself to serving the poor, the sick, and the marginalized, demonstrating the selfless love of Christ in his actions. His ministry was a reflection of his belief that God's love and power were available to all who sought them, regardless of their background or circumstances.

Despite facing many challenges and opposition during his ministry, Lake remained steadfast in his faith and commitment to serving God. He continued to travel and preach until his death on September 16, 1935, leaving behind a powerful legacy of faith, healing, and compassion.

And so, John Graham Lake was a true pioneer in the field of Christian healing and ministry. His unwavering faith, dedication to serving others, and belief in the power of God's love and healing continue to inspire Christians around the world. Lake's life and ministry serve as a reminder of the transformative power of faith and the boundless love of God for all humankind.

However, for this historical narrative, let's take again Lake's life story and ministry slowly, and see how he influenced the Apostolic Faith Mission of South Africa and it's offshoots. Influencers are usually students of other influencers too. Who could have influenced him in the first place?

The early 20th century saw the rise of influential figures who shaped the theological landscape of the Apostolic Faith Mission (AFM). Notable among them were Joseph Seymour (1906) and Charles Fox Parham (1900), founders of Bethel Bible College, who laid the groundwork for the Pentecostal movement.

However, it was John Alexander Dowie (1847-1907) who significantly impacted John G. Lake's theology. Dowie, a Scottish-born preacher, is revered as the "Healing Apostle" in Pentecostal-Charismatic circles.

Dowie's life was marked by a deep hunger for God's word. He read the Bible from Genesis to Revelation continuously, grounding his teachings in biblical texts. As a chaplain in Edinburgh, he interacted with medical professionals, often attending their presentations and observing the limitations of medical science in healing patients. This led him to pray against the medical fraternity's approach and instead pray for patients, resulting in remarkable healings.

In Newton, a devastating plague killed many, prompting Dowie to enhance his prayer life. He presided over 40 funerals in two weeks, but his faith remained unshaken. Instead, he intensified his prayers, and people were healed of various illnesses. Dowie's teachings emphasized divine healing, and his influence extended globally, from Australia to the USA.

When Dowie relocated to America, he was mightily used by God in healing and prophecy. His remarkable gifts earned him an invitation to the White House in 1901 by President William McKinley. During his visit, Dowie prophesied to the president about a vision he had received, warning of an assassination attempt and urging him to increase his security measures. Unfortunately, his warning was ignored.

Tragically, on September 6, 1901, President McKinley was assassinated in Buffalo, New York, while attending the Pan-American Exposition. Dowie's prophecy was later published in numerous newspapers, leaving many, including skeptical journalists, amazed and stunned.

John Graham Lake's personal life also experienced the power of healing through Alexander Dowie, a Scottish-American evangelist. When Lake's wife suffered from heart problems, they visited Dowie, who prayed for her healing. She was instantly cured. Lake then brought his two ailing brothers to Dowie, and they too were healed through his prayers.

From then on, Lake regularly attended Dowie's services and received the healing impartation from him. Inspired by Dowie's teachings, Lake adopted the practice of praying for healing instead of relying on medical assistance. After work, he would go door-to-door, praying and healing the sick, spreading the message of faith and divine healing.

However, as John Alexander Dowie's fame reached its peak, a series of unfortunate events began to unfold in his ministry. It is uncertain whether pride played a role, but the consequences were undeniable. Many of his people had prophesied that the spirit of Elijah rested upon Dowie, which may have contributed to his growing ego.

Initially, Dowie's ministry was centered on Christ, with the banner "Christ is All" being a hallmark of his teachings. However, as time passed, he began to shift his focus towards the Second Coming of Jesus Christ, linking it to the establishment of Zion City. He started dressing in elaborate robes and crowns, emulating the prophet Elijah.

Unfortunately, Dowie's desire for power and control led him down a path of corruption. He began embezzling funds and engaging in fraudulent activities, including underhanded sales of stands and houses in Zion City. His financial dealings became increasingly shady, attracting the attention of law enforcement.

As the authorities closed in, Dowie suffered a debilitating stroke, marking the beginning of his downfall. His once-promising ministry ended in disgrace, marred by scandal and controversy.

John G. Lake, who had been influenced by Dowie's teachings, appears to have taken up the mantle, distancing himself from later excesses and focusing on the core message of faith and healing. Despite Dowie's tragic end, his early teachings continued to inspire and shape the Pentecostal movement.

And so, John Alexander Dowie, a highly influential figure, significantly shaped John Lake's ministry, and his teachings had a lasting impact on Lake's theology and the doctrine of the Apostolic Faith Mission (AFM).

Dowie's legacy, in particular, continues to inspire and influence generations of faith leaders. His emphasis on divine healing, faith, and the power of prayer resonated deeply with Lake, who adopted these teachings and made them a central part of his own ministry.

One of the most controversial aspects of Lake's teachings, inherited from Dowie, was the rejection of medical assistance. This doctrinal position, which held that believers should rely solely on prayer and faith for healing, was a clear and unwavering stance under both Dowie and Lake's leadership. Additionally, certain practices like eating pork were considered taboo.

Although this stance on medical assistance has been a subject of debate within the AFM, both in its early years and currently, it remains a testament to the enduring influence of Dowie's teachings on Lake and the broader Pentecostal movement. While the AFM's position on medical assistance may have evolved over time, the legacy of Dowie and Lake's emphasis on faith and divine healing continues to shape the theology and practices of the movement.

Other 20th century influential figures who shaped the theological landscape of the Apostolic Faith Mission (AFM) were Joseph Seymour (1906), and Charles Fox Parham (1900), founder of Bethel Bible College.

Simultaneously, two influential mentorship relationships were unfolding. On one hand, John Graham Lake was understudying John Alexander Dowie, learning from his teachings and ministry. Meanwhile, on the other hand, William Joseph Seymour was understudying Charles Fox Parham, absorbing his insights and spiritual emphasis. Although they were geographically apart, these mentorship relationships would later converge to shape the course of the Pentecostal movement. Seymour would play a key role in the Azusa Street Revival, a pivotal event in the history of Pentecostalism, while John Graham Lake would go on to found the Apostolic Faith Mission of South Africa.

Although John Alexander Dowie and Charles Fox Parham are not entirely absent from the equation, they are viewed as distant influences on the Apostolic Faith Mission of South Africa. In contrast, William Joseph Seymour and John G. Lake play a more prominent role in the movement's history. Notably, John G. Lake was mentored by William Joseph Seymour, who is considered the founder of the Apostolic Faith Mission. This direct mentorship relationship solidifies Seymour's and Lake's central positions in the movement's development.

However, despite the distant influence of Dowie and Parham, the Apostolic Faith Mission in Zimbabwe recognizes a broader heritage of church fathers. According to their church law, under the section "Heritage", the renowned church fathers include:

- Charles Parham and William Seymour in America
- Tom Hezmalhalch and John Graham Lake in South Africa
- Zacharias Manamela and Kgobe in Gobatema, Gwanda, in southwestern Zimbabwe

This acknowledgment highlights the diverse roots and influences that have shaped the Apostolic Faith Mission in Zimbabwe, extending beyond the primary figures of Seymour and Lake.

Notably, the only figure not mentioned in the Apostolic Faith Mission in Zimbabwe's constitution under the "Heritage" section is John Alexander Dowie. This omission may be due to his lack of direct connection to the Azusa Street Revival, which played a pivotal role in the movement's foundation. Alternatively, it could be attributed to Dowie's decline in influence and vigor during his later years, which may have diminished his impact on the movement's development.

Another indirect influential figure in John Graham Lake's ministry was Charles Fox Parham, through William Seymour.

William Joseph Seymour, an African American man who lived with a disability in one eye, was a premature graduate of Bethel College. Despite his physical limitations, Seymour was deeply passionate about the work of the Holy Spirit, which was a central focus of the college's teachings. During his time at Bethel, students were assigned to research the New Testament Bible to identify scriptural bases for the fruits and works of the Holy Spirit. This research yielded five key examples in the Bible where the Holy Spirit manifested following specific events:

1. Acts 2:4 - The outpouring of the Holy Spirit on the day of Pentecost

2. Acts 8:17 - The laying on of hands by Peter and John to receive the Holy Spirit

3. Acts 9:17 - The scales falling from Paul's eyes, symbolizing his reception of the Holy Spirit

4. Acts 10:44 (&45) - The Holy Spirit falling on the Gentiles, marking a significant turning point in the early Christian church

5. Acts 19:6 - The Holy Spirit coming upon the Ephesian disciples, accompanied by speaking in tongues and prophesying

These scriptures became foundational to the doctrine of the Holy Spirit and later influenced the establishment of the Apostolic Faith Mission of South Africa, albeit indirectly through John G. Lake, who never met Charles Parham but was influenced by Seymour's teachings.

On January 1, 1901, a remarkable event occurred at Bethel College, where Agnes N. Ozman became the first person to speak in tongues, speaking in Chinese for three days and writing in Chinese. Parham and others also experienced speaking in tongues, marking a significant milestone in the development of modern Pentecostalism. Although Seymour had already left the college by then, his teachings and legacy continued to shape the movement. Parham is widely regarded as the father of modern Pentecostalism, and his influence extended far beyond Bethel College, shaping the course of Christian history. Charles Parham is credited with coining the term "AFM" for the Apostolic Faith Movement, and his legacy as the founder of the movement is forever commemorated on his tombstone, which bears an inscription testifying to his pioneering role.

Who was this William Joseph Seymour, mightily used by God? Seymour a pivotal figure in the history of the Pentecostal movement in the United States, was born on May 2, 1870, in Centerville, Louisiana. Despite facing racial discrimination and segregation in the post-Civil War South, Seymour felt called to ministry and pursued his faith with fervor. In 1906, he led a small prayer group in Los Angeles, which grew into the Azusa Street Revival, a focal point of the emerging Pentecostal movement. Seymour's leadership emphasized the experience of the Holy Spirit and speaking in tongues, shaping Pentecostal theology. He also welcomed people of all races, establishing Pentecostalism as a multiracial and multicultural movement.

The Azusa Street Revival had a far-reaching impact, spreading Pentecostalism globally through missionaries and believers who visited. Seymour's legacy as a pioneering figure continues to resonate, emphasizing the experience of the Holy Spirit, racial inclusivity, and challenging established theological norms.

Although Seymour faced challenges, including criticism, personal struggles, and financial difficulties, his resilience and steadfast faith enabled him to overcome them. His belief in the transforming power of the Holy Spirit inspired countless individuals to embrace Pentecostalism.

And so, William Joseph Seymour was a visionary leader whose impact on the Pentecostal movement is immeasurable. His leadership and commitment to the experience of the Holy Spirit and racial inclusivity have left a lasting mark on Christianity, serving as a testament to the power of faith, perseverance, and the transformative work of the Holy Spirit.

To conclude the American chapter of the AFM, let's explore the Revival briefly. The Azusa Street Revival (1906-1909) marked a pivotal moment in Pentecostal history, with the Holy Spirit moving powerfully for three days. People experienced diverse manifestations, including speaking in tongues, singing, laughing, groaning, and lying still, unceasingly. This revival duplicated, and perhaps even surpassed, the Day of Pentecost.

The Azusa Street Revival was a global phenomenon, launching many preachers into various parts of the world. Although the Apostolic Faith Mission (AFM) emerged from Azusa, it wasn't the only movement born from the revival.

The Four Square Gospel, which emphasized: 1. Jesus saves;

2. He baptizes with the Holy Spirit;

3. He heals;

4. He is coming back again, was a central teaching at Azusa. John G. Lake was exposed to this gospel before founding the AFM in Africa and taught the same to his followers. Lake's mentorship under William Seymour, who was influenced by Charles Parham, shaped his understanding of the Holy Spirit and healing.

And so, Lake inherited the emphasis on healing from John Alexander Dowie and the Pentecostal doctrine, including the baptism of the Holy Spirit evidenced by speaking in tongues, from Parham through Seymour. This legacy continues to influence the AFM and broader Pentecostal movement. John Graham Lake himself was baptized with the Holy Spirit in October 1907.

John G. Lake, a remarkable healing evangelist, witnessed several notable healing cases during his ministry. A woman who had been blind from birth regained her sight after he prayed for her. He also prayed for a man diagnosed with terminal cancer, and the man was completely cured. These are just a few examples of Lake's documented healings, which were publicly verified as genuine among the many he performed. Lake's ministry was characterized by signs, wonders, and supernatural encounters, leaving a lasting impact on those who followed his teachings.

The Apostolic Faith Movement has its roots in the early 20th century, with key figures playing a significant role in its development. Charles Fox Parham, an American evangelist, is credited with founding the Apostolic Faith Movement (AFM), in Topeka, Kansas, in 1901. This movement emphasized the importance of speaking in tongues as evidence of the Holy Spirit's baptism.

Meanwhile, William Joseph Seymour, an African American preacher, led the Azusa Street Revival in Los Angeles, California, in 1906. This revival became a catalyst for the global Pentecostal movement, and Seymour's congregation became known as the Apostolic Faith Mission (AFM), with a focus on Pentecostal teachings and practices.

In Africa, John Graham Lake, a Canadian-American missionary, arrived in South Africa in April 1908. He founded the Apostolic Faith Mission of South Africa (AFM) on May 25, 1908, in Doornfontein, Johannesburg. Lake's mission emphasized divine healing, evangelism, and the Pentecostal experience. The AFM of South Africa would go on to play a significant role in spreading Pentecostalism throughout the continent.

So, this is the background of the founder of the Church, Apostolic Faith Mission of South Africa. Initially, John G. Lake's intention was not to establish a church, but rather an evangelistic mission based on the Apostolic faith - the faith and teachings of the original Apostles. The mission aimed to spread the message of salvation, divine healing, and the Pentecostal experience. However, due to the South African government's administrative regulations, Lake was required to register the movement as a formal entity. Consequently, the Apostolic Faith Mission was registered, first as an unlimited company, then as a church. This transition from a mission to a church was largely driven by the need to comply with legal requirements, rather than a deliberate attempt to establish a new denomination.

CHAPTER three

Pioneering Faith: The Establishment of the Apostolic Faith Mission in South Africa

In a historic moment, a group of pioneering missionaries arrived in South Africa, eager to spread the gospel and establish the Apostolic Faith Mission (AFM) in the region. The team consisted of John G. Lake, his wife, and their seven children, accompanied by Mr. and Mrs. Hezmalhalch, Mr. Lehman, and Miss Sackett. This courageous group of individuals left behind the familiarity of their homes in the USA, driven by a shared vision to bring hope and salvation to the people of South Africa.

Notably, Mr. Lehman was the only member of the team with prior experience in Africa, having spent five years ministering to Black communities during a previous visit. His expertise and understanding of the local context proved invaluable as the team navigated the challenges of establishing a new mission in a foreign land. As they settled in South Africa, they were later joined by additional workers from the USA, who shared their passion for spreading the gospel and building a vibrant Christian community. Together, they laid the foundations for the AFM in South Africa, paving the way for a legacy of faith, hope, and transformation.

Upon arrival at Cape Town, they boarded a train to Johannesburg without a specific address or hotel reservations. The night before their arrival, God spoke to a woman named Mrs. C.L. Goodenough in a vision, instructing her to receive and care for a missionary team arriving the next day. Although she was not given their names, she was shown an image of the leader, John Graham Lake, in her dream.

As the train pulled into Johannesburg station on an April morning, Lake and his team were uncertain about their next steps. Meanwhile, Mrs. Goodenough waited at the station, trusting in the vision she had received. When Lake stepped off the train, Mrs. Goodenough immediately recognized him from her dream and ran to greet him. The reunion was marked by excitement, awe, and gratitude on both sides, as God's faithfulness and provision were evident.

Without delay, Lake and his team followed Mrs. Goodenough to their new home, where they would establish the Apostolic Faith Mission of South Africa. This remarkable story of divine guidance and provision set the stage for the mission's growth and impact across the continent.

When John G. Lake arrived in South Africa, he was welcomed by a small group of believers in Johannesburg apart from the initial welcome by Mrs Goodenough. He quickly began preaching and teaching about divine healing, salvation, and the Pentecostal experience, which resonated deeply with the people. His ministry rapidly gained attention, and he started conducting healing meetings and evangelistic campaigns, drawing large crowds and sparking both interest and controversy.

As his message and methods attracted many followers, Lake established the Apostolic Faith Mission in Johannesburg, on 25 May 1908, which became the headquarters of his ministry. Despite facing opposition and criticism from some religious leaders and the media, who were skeptical of his claims and methods, Lake continued to preach, teach, and heal, undeterred. His ministry expanded to other parts of South Africa, leaving a lasting impact on the country's religious landscape.

Lake's arrival marked the beginning of a new era in South African Christianity, characterized by a strong emphasis on divine healing, the Pentecostal experience, and evangelism. His legacy would continue to shape the country's religious landscape for generations to come.

Let's revisit this story at a slower pace, taking the time to absorb the details and significance of John G. Lake's arrival in South Africa and the subsequent events that unfolded.

John G Lake's decision to officially launch the Apostolic Faith Mission of South Africa on May 25, 1908, was likely influenced by his deep respect for his mentor, John Alexander Dowie. Dowie, a Scottish-American evangelist, had a profound impact on Lake's understanding of the healing ministry. Lake regarded Dowie as his first serious mentor in the healing ministry, and Dowie's teachings and example played a significant role in shaping Lake's approach to divine healing.

Furthermore, Lake's experience at the Azusa Street Revival in 1906, led by William Joseph Seymour, was instrumental in equipping him for the healing ministry. Seymour's emphasis on the Holy Spirit's empowerment and the manifestation of spiritual gifts, including healing, had a profound impact on Lake. The Azusa Street Revival was a pivotal moment in the development of the Pentecostal movement, and Lake's involvement with Seymour's ministry helped prepare him for his own missionary work in South Africa.

Given the significance of Dowie's influence on Lake's life and ministry, it is likely that Lake chose May 25 as the official launch date for the AFM of South Africa to honor his mentor. May 25 was a meaningful day for Dowie, and Lake's decision to begin his ministry on this date may have been a way of acknowledging Dowie's impact on his life and work. By launching the AFM on this date, Lake was, in effect, continuing Dowie's legacy and building upon the foundation laid by his mentor.

John Alexander Dowie was born on May 25, 1847. This is likely the reason why May 25 held significance for John G. Lake, as mentioned earlier. Lake's decision to launch the Apostolic Faith Mission of South Africa on May 25, 1908, was probably a deliberate choice to honor his mentor's birthday.

Considering that Sunday, May 24, 1908, was a day of worship for most Christians, including the Apostolic Faith Mission of South Africa, it would have been logical for John G. Lake and his team to establish the church on that day. Instead, Lake chose to launch the AFM of South Africa on Monday, May 25, 1908, a day that didn't hold significant religious importance for the church. This decision suggests that Lake was motivated by a personal reason, likely honoring his mentor John Alexander Dowie's birthday, which was on May 25.

It's possible that Lake didn't explicitly share this reason with his colleagues, but the deliberate choice of May 25 as the establishment date implies a personal significance. An alternative explanation could be that May 25 was the day the church was officially registered with the South African government, rather than the day of its spiritual inception. However, the coincidence of the date with Dowie's birthday implies a deeper meaning behind Lake's decision.

The Apostolic Faith Mission of South Africa experienced exponential growth, with tens of thousands of converts joining the movement in a remarkably short period. To put this into perspective, John G. Lake arrived in South Africa with a team of around 16 preachers (including those who arrived later), who were responsible for following up on new assemblies and providing pastoral care to the burgeoning flock. Meanwhile, Lake pressed on, establishing at least two new assemblies every week, as he preached the "Four-Square Gospel": Jesus saves, baptizes with the Holy Spirit, heals, and is coming back again.

This rapid expansion was not solely focused on building a church, but rather on spreading the message of salvation and the Pentecostal experience. As noted earlier, the minutes from 1908 reveal that Lake's initial intention was not to establish a church, but rather to conduct an evangelistic mission. The name "Apostolic Faith Mission" was more a descriptive term for their work than a formal denominational title. Lake's emphasis was on preaching the gospel, healing the sick, and empowering believers with the Holy Spirit, rather than building a traditional church structure. This approach allowed the movement to remain flexible and focused on its core mission, as it rapidly expanded across South Africa.

The practice of holding elections within the Apostolic Faith Mission (AFM) is not a recent development, but rather a tradition that dates back to the church's early years in South Africa. In fact, the first elections were held on 27 May 1908, the same year the church was established. Although the presiding officer's identity is unknown, the minutes of that election, which elected Thomas Hezelmulch as the first president of the AFM of South Africa, are well-preserved in the church library. Notably, John G. Lake served as the church's vice president.

However, Lake's tenure was short-lived, as he returned to the United States in 1913, just five years after arriving in Africa. To his credit, he left behind 125 functional white assemblies and 500 functional black assemblies.

In 1918 or 1919, LeRoux succeeded John Lake, who had himself succeeded Tom Hezelmulch as the AFM president, serving for approximately 30 years until stepping down due to age in 1942/3.

Interestingly, the AFM experienced its first split in 1909, when John Lake became president, and Thomas Hezelmulch returned to America. This event highlights that splits within the church are not a recent phenomenon, but rather a recurring aspect of its history. The split within the Apostolic Faith Mission (AFM) in 1908, resulting in the resignation of President Thomas Hezmalhalch less than a year into his tenure, remains a sensitive topic that few people care to discuss. Some may attribute the reluctance to revisit this episode to Hezmalhalch's decision to quietly step down and return home, rather than engaging in a public dispute. Others might downplay the incident as merely a disagreement that led to his resignation, glossing over the underlying tensions and conflicts that ultimately drove the split.

However, it is essential to acknowledge the significance of this event in the AFM's history, as it marked a pivotal moment in the church's development. The circumstances surrounding Hezmalhalch's resignation, including the power struggles and theological disagreements that contributed to the split, continue to shape the AFM's trajectory and inform its leadership dynamics to this day. By examining this episode in greater detail, we can gain a deeper understanding of the complex factors that have influenced the AFM's evolution over time.

The second significant split occurred around 1914/5, soon after the departure of John G Lake back to America, when Lekganyane, the founder of the Zion Christian Church (ZCC) with head conference center at Morija, Petersburg, in South Africa, and Samuel Moyo (later known as Mutendi), the founder of ZCC in Zimbabwe, parted ways with the AFM. The name "Zion" was linked to John Alexander Dowie of Zion City, who established the Zionistic teachings and emphasis.

As we delve deeper into the history of the Apostolic Faith Mission (AFM), we will examine the splits and divisions that have occurred within the organization. However, it is essential to note that pride has often been a detrimental factor, hindering individuals from reaching their full potential. This phenomenon is evident in the AFM's history, particularly in the conflict between John Lake and his co-missionary Thomas Hezelmalch. The conflict has been conveniently glossed over and virtually erased from memory, as if it never happened. In a striking example of selective remembrance, John Lake is often solely credited and revered as the pioneering figure of the Apostolic Faith Mission (AFM) of South Africa, while the contributions and roles of others, including Thomas Hezelmalch, are seemingly forgotten or deliberately omitted. This skewed narrative has effectively airbrushed the controversy from the AFM's history, leaving a sanitized version that neglects the complexities and challenges faced by the organization. By doing so, the AFM's story is reduced to a simplistic and incomplete account that fails to acknowledge the intricacies of its past.

Interestingly, just as the Bible says, "one reaps what they sow," and "do to others what you would like them to do to you (Matthew 7:12)," many members and leaders who have broken away from the AFM tend to distance themselves from the organization and its history. In their biographies and accounts, there is often a conspicuous absence of any mention of their time in the AFM, as if they never belonged to the church. This omission suggests a desire to disassociate themselves from the conflicts and controversies that have marred the AFM's history.

This pattern of behavior is not unique to the AFM, as pride and the desire for independence can lead individuals to downplay or deny their past affiliations. However, by acknowledging and learning from the past, we can gain valuable insights into the complexities of human nature and the challenges of building and maintaining a unified community.

In the context of the AFM, the splits and divisions have resulted in the formation of new churches and organizations, each with their own distinct identity and mission. While these developments have contributed to the diversification of the Pentecostal landscape, they also underscore the need for humility, forgiveness, and reconciliation within the body of Christ.

Just as the origins of evil can be traced back to the Garden of Eden, where humanity's first disobedience occurred, the redemptive plan of God also began to unfold in the same sacred space. Similarly, the seeds of division and splintering within the Apostolic Faith Mission (AFM) were sown at its inception in 1908. This pivotal year saw Thomas Hezelmalch, a key figure in the AFM's early days, depart for America, marking the first significant rift in the church's unity. Shortly thereafter, two Zionist colleagues broke away to establish their own distinct Zion Churches, diverging from John Alexander Dowie's original Zionist church in South Africa.

While these schisms ultimately contributed to the growth of the Universal Church of Jesus Christ, the visible church, particularly the Apostolic Faith Mission, has experienced a tumultuous journey marked by periods of involution, spiritual stagnation, and decline. These challenges have had far-reaching consequences, impacting the spiritual lives of numerous members across generations. The remedy for these divisions and struggles must be sought in the same era, acknowledging the complex interplay between historical events, human actions, and divine providence.

At times, the church has deviated from God's plan by appointing leaders based on human wisdom, rather than divine guidance. A notable example is the election of Matthias to replace Judas Iscariot (Acts 1:23-26). While the disciples prayed and cast lots, seeking God's direction, they had already narrowed down the selection to two candidates, Joseph Barsabbas and Matthias. However, this process raises questions about the extent of God's involvement. What if neither of the chosen candidates was truly worthy of the position? The fact that Matthias is not mentioned again in the New Testament, unlike Paul, who was divinely chosen as an apostle despite being an unlikely candidate, suggests that God may not have been directly involved in Matthias' selection. In contrast, Paul's story continues to inspire and guide believers to this day, highlighting the importance of seeking God's true guidance in leadership appointments.

The primary cause of spiritual stagnation in today's church is the prevalence of leaders who, despite their prominent positions, are not genuinely chosen by God. Instead, many are mere human appointments, masquerading as divinely ordained leaders. Like whitewashed tombs, they appear outwardly impressive but lack the inner substance of true spiritual calling and anointing. As a result, only a small minority of leaders in key positions are truly God's choice, leaving the rest to perpetuate a facade of spirituality that ultimately hinders the church's growth and effectiveness.

Jesus Christ declared that whatever the church binds on earth will be bound in heaven (Matthew 16:19, 18:18). However, this statement raises important questions. Did Jesus intend to imply that human decisions can override God's will? Or did He mean that the church's actions should align with divine guidance? It seems contradictory to suggest that Christ would advocate for shutting out God's interventions in church affairs. Yet, when church regulations neglect the role of prophecy and the spoken word of God, it creates a void in allowing God to intervene in church elections.

The Apostolic Faith Mission, which professes to believe in a vocal God, appears to contradict this conviction by maintaining constitutions and regulations that effectively silence God's voice. By prioritizing human decision-making over divine guidance, the church risks neglecting the very essence of its faith. If the church truly believes in a God who speaks, it must create space for His voice to be heard, especially in critical matters like leadership elections.

CHAPTER four

From South Africa to Zimbabwe: The Expansion of the Apostolic Faith Mission

The Apostolic Faith Mission's crusades in South Africa attracted numerous immigrants from Southern Rhodesia (now Zimbabwe), particularly from Matabeleland South. Written records indicate that many of these individuals were deeply impacted by the message, converting to Christianity and receiving baptism with the Holy Spirit. In December 1908, they returned to Zimbabwe, eager to share the Pentecostal Four-Square Gospel with their communities.

The gospel message thrived in Matabeleland South and beyond, as local Zimbabweans also received the message and were baptized with the Holy Spirit. Notably, John G. Lake's teachings emphasized the importance of receiving the Holy Spirit's baptism before water baptism if no water-baptizer was available, reflecting his orthodox and orthoprax approach. Lake believed that speaking in tongues was a non-negotiable evidence of the Holy Spirit's baptism, and every believer was expected to manifest this gift.

To foster an environment of spiritual fervor, the Apostolic Faith Mission designated every Wednesday as a prayer and fasting service, where believers would gather to seek God's presence and empowerment. This practice, known as a "tarrying service," was later referred to by some as a "tearring service." It was a time when the community would come together to fervently seek God, crying out for a more profound experience of the Holy Spirit's power and presence in their lives. The term "tarrying" emphasizes the act of waiting and lingering in prayer, while "tearring" conveys a sense of intense, passionate crying out to God. Despite the variation in terminology, the essence of the practice remained the same – a collective, heartfelt pursuit of a deeper spiritual experience. Through these services, the church experienced a profound sense of unity and spiritual growth, as believers continued to seek the fullness of the Holy Spirit.

And so, to be exact and true, the Apostolic Faith Mission (AFM) arrived in Zimbabwe in 1908, during the Christmas season, approximately six months after its official launch in South Africa on May 25, 1908.

This pioneering work predates the arrival of any Pentecostal missionaries in Southern Rhodesia, making it a groundbreaking moment in the region's religious history. The events and developments that followed are meticulously documented in the minutes and reports of the Zimbabwean mission of the Apostolic Faith Mission (AFM) of South Africa, which are archived in the church library in South Africa.

This marked the beginning of a gradual growth period, which would ultimately lead to the official launch of the AFM in Zimbabwe seven years later, in 1915.

As mentioned earlier, initial introduction of the AFM to Zimbabwe was facilitated by immigrant workers who had returned home for the Christmas holidays, bringing with them the Pentecostal message they had received in South Africa. This spontaneous spread of the gospel laid the foundation for the eventual establishment of the AFM in Zimbabwe.

Over the next seven years, the AFM continued to grow and consolidate its presence in Zimbabwe, with missionaries like Dugmore and Manamela playing a crucial role in reinforcing the work of local pioneers and expanding the mission's reach. The official launch of the AFM in Zimbabwe in 1915 marked a significant milestone in the history of the church, recognizing its established presence and commitment to spreading the Pentecostal message in the region.

In response to reports that the people of Matabeleland had received the gospel and been baptized with the Holy Spirit through the efforts of immigrant workers who had returned home for Christmas, Missionary Dugmore was dispatched to the region. On arrival, he led the first official service at the home of Lukas Mutokwa, a Tswana resident, marking a significant milestone in the establishment of the Apostolic Faith Mission (AFM) in Zimbabwe.

Notably, the boundary between Botswana and Zimbabwe was not strictly defined at the time, and communities along the border shared cultural and social ties, much like today. This fluidity allowed for seamless interactions and the spread of the gospel across the region.

The service at Lukas Mutokwa's home, documented in the records of the AFM of South Africa, marked the beginning of regular weekly and midweek gatherings. This assembly, established in Mutokwa's home, served as a hub for spiritual growth, fellowship, and evangelism, paving the way for the expansion of the AFM in Zimbabwe. Today, the AFM library in Johannesburg houses documented evidence of this historic event, testifying to the missionary efforts and the receptivity of the people to the Pentecostal message.

However, the individual tasked with securing recognition from the Rhodesian colonial authorities was Rev. G.J. Booysen, based in Louis Trichardt. It is likely that Rev. Booysen worked under the supervision of Dugmore, given that Zachariah Manamela also reported to him, suggesting a hierarchical structure within the organization.

In 1909, Zachariah Manamela, a dedicated missionary of Malawian origin, emerged as a key figure in the Apostolic Faith Mission (AFM) of South Africa's Southern Rhodesia mission. According to the workers' council minutes of 1909, Manamela was officially entrusted with leading the mission under the supervision of Missionary Dugmore. Although the minutes do not specify his exact office, ministry, or official role, it is clear that Manamela was a valued member of the AFM of South Africa, deployed to Matabeleland South to reinforce the pioneering work of local evangelists who had introduced the gospel during the 1908 festive season.

Manamela's contributions were significant, as he not only consolidated the existing work but also established additional branch assemblies, expanding the mission's reach beyond the main assembly headquartered at Lukas Mutokwa's house. His efforts ensured the continued growth and spread of the Pentecostal message in the region, building upon the foundations laid by the initial group of immigrant workers who had shared the gospel with their communities. Through Manamela's leadership and dedication, the AFM of South Africa's presence in Southern Rhodesia was solidified, paving the way for further expansion and evangelization in the years to come.

Zachariah Manamela, a devoted follower of John Graham Lake, embraced the teachings and practices inherited from John Alexander Dowie, including dietary restrictions based on Leviticus 11 and 14. Specifically, Manamela adhered to the belief that certain foods, such as pork and unclean insects like mopane worms or mopane caterpillars (Gonimbrasia belina), were forbidden.

However, this stance conflicted with the local culture in Matabeleland South, where mopane worms are a traditional delicacy and staple relish.

As a result, Manamela's strict adherence to these dietary laws led to tension with the local community, ultimately resulting in his expulsion by Chief Nhlamba around the 1910-1911 season. The historical records, maintained by white missionaries who focused primarily on the mission field rather than the workers, simply note that Manamela "proceeded to the north of Matabeleland South" without providing further details about his relocation or subsequent activities.

This lack of documentation may contribute to Manamela's relative obscurity in the history of the Apostolic Faith Mission, as the records prioritize the mission's activities over the experiences and contributions of individual workers like Manamela. Nevertheless, his commitment to the teachings of Lake and Dowie demonstrates the significant influence of these early Pentecostal leaders on the development of the AFM in Southern Africa.

Following the departure of Zachariah Manamela, Mr. Ngcobe assumed his role, continuing to serve under the leadership of Rev. G.J. Booysen, just as Manamela had done previously. Notably, Mr. Ngcobe possessed the remarkable gift of divine healing, and he exercised this gift through faith healing, bringing hope and restoration to those in need.

In the library records spanning 1913-1915, we find accounts of Missionary Dugmore's return to Matabeleland South, specifically the Gobatema area, with the goal of establishing the first-ever mission station in Southern Rhodesia. This pioneering effort led to the founding of the Gobatema Mission, with the Apostolic Faith Mission of South Africa holding the title deeds to the property.

In 1919, following a protracted struggle with local authorities, the Apostolic Faith Mission (AFM) successfully acquired the Gobatema Farm, located south of Gwanda, and established it as a strategic base for its missionary operations. This pivotal milestone marked a significant expansion of the AFM's reach and influence in the region, enabling the organization to further its gospel work and community outreach.

Despite repeated efforts, the Apostolic Faith Mission of South Africa faced prolonged delays in securing official recognition from the Zimbabwean authorities, due to a complex array of factors and circumstances. Undeterred in his pursuit of official recognition, David Bosman relocated from Johannesburg to Matabeleland in 1925, dedicating himself to securing formal acknowledgment for the Apostolic Faith Mission (AFM) in the region. His primary focus was to consolidate and expand the mission's work, centered on the strategic Gobatema Farm, which had been established as a key operations base six years earlier. By concentrating efforts on this hub, Bosman aimed to strengthen the AFM's presence and impact in Matabeleland.

The quest for recognition and registration continued to face obstacles, hindering progress in this area. A significant setback occurred in June 1932, when Louis L. Kruger and Harris's application for recognition as Missionary Superintendents was rejected. Consequently, plans to establish schools were put on hold. In fact, the already operational Gobatema School was forced to close due to the missionaries' lack of adequate educational qualifications, as noted by the Inspector of the Native Development Department on June 22, 1932.

Undeterred, Swanepoel secretly reopened a school at Gobatema in 1934, but it was discovered and shut down by the government in June 1936. Two years later, W. Wilson was still struggling to establish a school, and in a letter to authorities, he mentioned that the Mission intended to replace its European overseers with better-qualified individuals. On September 24, 1938, the Native Commissioner responded, stating that the application for a village school at Gobatema would be considered once the Mission met the government's requirements for European supervision.

In a follow-up letter in August 1938, Wilson informed the authorities that the unqualified European Overseers were being transferred from Rhodesia to Johannesburg by the Mission's Headquarters. This personnel change may have included L. Kruger, as there is little mention of him after 1938.

As a result, the church was faced with a difficult decision in its pursuit of recognition and registration. To meet the government's requirements, it had to replace the spirit-filled missionaries, who were called by God but lacked formal qualifications, with individuals who possessed government-approved credentials. This shift led to the introduction of missionaries who, although qualified by human standards, often lacked the zeal and spiritual fervor that had characterized the Apostolic Faith Mission of South Africa's early years. This compromise would have far-reaching consequences, as the church's leadership prioritized institutional legitimacy over spiritual intensity. We will delve deeper into the implications of this decision and its impact on the church's trajectory in a subsequent narrative.

The prolonged struggle for recognition finally came to an end with the successful registration of the Apostolic Faith Mission by Enoch Gwanzura in 1943. This milestone followed a tumultuous journey, marked by the initial registration in 1931 by Louis Krugar, only to be revoked in 1934 due to alleged inconsistencies, as deemed by the government at the time. The revocation led to a nine-year delay, ultimately resolved by Gwanzura's efforts, securing the church's official status.

Matabeleland South was home to several prominent figures in the early days of the Apostolic Faith Mission (AFM) of South Africa, including Paulos Mbulawa and Joseph Madumeja, who were ordained in 1916 as among the first preachers, ministers, or evangelists in the Native Church of the AFM of South Africa within Southern Rhodesia. Other notable evangelists of the time included Mabhanga, Bhengu, and several others. Mbulawa and Madumeja were instrumental in covering the entire region of Matabeleland, using bicycles as their primary mode of transportation. Photographs of the two evangelists on bicycles can be found in the AFM of South Africa's library, featured in the church magazine, where they were referred to as "evangelists".

During that era, native pastors underwent brief training before being ordained as evangelists, rather than elders. Their certificates specifically stated "evangelist", as the term "pastor" was reserved for white individuals, based on their interpretation of Ephesians 4:11. Despite this, these early evangelists fulfilled roles equivalent to modern-day pastors. Today, elders are still referred to as evangelists, maintaining a connection to the native pastors of the early and mid-1900s. However, it is essential to acknowledge that these pioneering evangelists were, in fact, pastors in the modern sense, playing a vital role in shaping the church's history in the region.

The AFM of South Africa library records also detail the contributions made by various individuals towards the establishment of the mission, including the purchase of the farm. Notably, another missionary, Golden, arrived to support the work, but tragically succumbed to malaria after only two years of service. His legacy lives on, however, through the tomb erected in his memory, located less than a kilometer from the church, bearing the inscription "Missionary Golden" and the year of his passing, 1917.

This sequence of events marks the significant milestone of the Apostolic Faith Mission of South Africa's expansion into Southern Rhodesia (now Zimbabwe). The establishment of the Gobatema Mission served as a foothold for further evangelization and growth, paving the way for the AFM's continued presence in the region. The sacrifices made by missionaries like Golden underscore the challenges and dedication required to spread the gospel in uncharted territories.

This narrative seeks to explore the profound impact of the Apostolic Faith Mission of South Africa's history in Zimbabwe on the current state and operations of the church. Although the Apostolic Faith Mission in Zimbabwe has gained autonomy and independence from its parent church in South Africa, a critical question remains: has it successfully transitioned beyond the legacy of segregation and discrimination that characterized its past? Specifically, has the church fully liberated itself from the shackles of racial, social, political, and educational segregation that historically defined its existence? Or do remnants of these norms still influence its leadership, membership, and community engagement? By examining the church's evolution and current practices, this narrative aims to uncover the extent to which the Apostolic Faith Mission in Zimbabwe has overcome its complex history and forged a truly inclusive and equitable path forward.

CHAPTER five

Navigating Complexities: The AFM's Story in Zimbabwe

On June 20, 1918, Pieter Luttig established himself in Kadoma as an AFM representative, aiming to evangelize the local African township and mining compounds. He baptized his first African convert, Solomon, on February 12, 1919. Seeking to expand his reach, Luttig hired John Wesley Dingiswayo, a charismatic preacher with a troubled past, including allegations of financial dishonesty and adultery. However, their partnership was short-lived due to Luttig's decision to rebaptize Methodist church members without consulting their parent body, sparking protests from the Methodist synod. A formal complaint was lodged with the Chief Native Commissioner and AFM headquarters, citing a breach of protocol. In response, D. Bosman relieved Luttig of his duties and appointed T.H.M. Bates, who worked diligently until 1926. S. Harris from South Africa then succeeded Bates, continuing the mission work in Kadoma.

This incident highlights the challenges faced by early missionaries in navigating complex relationships with local communities, other denominations, and their own headquarters. Luttig's actions, although well-intentioned, demonstrate the importance of collaboration and communication in missionary work.

The incident involving Luttig and Dingiswayo reveals a nuanced dynamic within the Apostolic Faith Mission (AFM) during the colonial era. Contrary to assumptions, white missionaries like Luttig were not inherently segregationalists, but rather, they were often victims of circumstance, navigating a complex web of colonial politics and social norms. They feared that any misstep could provoke the colonial government to take decisive action against them, jeopardizing their missionary work.

Dingiswayo's dismissal from the Methodist Church due to personal conduct didn't stop the Methodist synod from contacting AFM headquarters to express discontent with Luttig's actions. This move aimed to frustrate Luttig's successful ministry, which attracted Methodist congregants to be rebaptized. The synod prioritized protecting its interests over supporting the Gospel's spread. Despite opposition, Luttig's ministry thrived, with many

Africans embracing his message, revealing a deep hunger for spiritual truth and need for inclusive leadership. This episode highlights complex dynamics between missionaries, local communities, and colonial authorities, showing even well-intentioned individuals like Luttig faced significant challenges.

Native Church Overseer D. Bosman showed wise leadership by temporarily replacing Luttig with local interim T.H.M. Bates, while seeking a permanent solution. Bosman aimed to find a white missionary to succeed Luttig and a qualified black leader to replace Dingiswayo, previously employed by Luttig. After a thorough search, Bosman appointed S. Harris, a seasoned white missionary, and Isaac Chiumbu, an educated and capable black leader. This dynamic duo was equipped to assume the responsibilities previously shared by Luttig and Dingiswayo, bringing stability and continuity to the AFM's mission in Kadoma.

Isaac Chiumbu had just relocated from South Africa to Kadoma, accompanied by his employer, Laurell, (the local Shona and Nyanja people, not able to pronounce well his name called him, Ruru). Laurell had recently secured a position as a department manager at Cam and Motor Mine. Notably, both Chiumbu and Laurell had previously experienced the baptism of the Holy Spirit, characterized by speaking in tongues, while still in South Africa. Although Laurell was a member of the whites-only AFM church in Kadoma, he often attended native church gatherings alongside S Harris, who was involved in an official capacity. Through Harris' connections, Laurell was able to engage with the native church community, fostering a unique opportunity for cross-cultural exchange and spiritual growth.

The simultaneous relocation of Harris and Laurell from South Africa may have been a strategic move orchestrated by Native Church Overseer D. Bosman. This arrangement would have enabled Harris to assume leadership of the Kadoma church region, while Laurell's cook, Isaac Chiumbu, could be utilized for essential interpretation and secretarial support at the Native Church in Rimuka, thereby optimizing resources and expertise within the church network.

Harris brought valuable experience and expertise, while Chiumbu provided essential local knowledge and cultural understanding. Together, they formed a formidable team, capable of navigating the complexities of the African context and advancing the Gospel. Bosman's thoughtful approach ensured a seamless transition, allowing the AFM to maintain its momentum and continue its vital work in the region.

The Apostolic Faith Mission (AFM) headquarters was initially located in Gwanda town until the arrival of Louis L. Krugar in 1929/30 at Gobatema. Krugar's mission was to conduct a census of believers, register the church with the Southern Rhodesian government, and establish a missionary operations base in the capital. He was accompanied by a group of missionaries and later relocated the headquarters to Harare (then Salisbury) to be closer to the central government authorities and take advantage of the city's strategic transportation and communication links.

During this time, my grandfather, a young member of the church, became increasingly involved in church administration and ministry. A decision was made to establish Southern Rhodesia as a separate mission field, with Louis L. Kruger as the overseer, and Salisbury as the new central hub. Gwanda and Gatooma were designated as related districts, with Louis L. Kruger based in Salisbury, while Harris and Isaac Chiumbu worked in Gatooma (Kadoma) townships and neighboring chiefdoms.

Meanwhile, in the eastern part of the country, a railway employee named Holtzhausen introduced AFM to Mutare, from where Pentecostalism spread to Rusape and Wedza. These developments are documented in the report compiled by Louis L. Kruger, detailing the progress of AFM's Zimbabwean chapter.

Krugar was accompanied by an interpreter, Shonhihwa Masedza (who later founded Johane Masowe, not Johane Masowe Chishanu, but the original tinsmiths and basket makers). He was a key man, assistant to Louis Krugar, ordained as an evangelist, or native pastor on 26 June 1933.

Masedza was a renowned and dynamic preacher, endowed with a powerful charismatic gift that brought healing to countless individuals. He was esteemed alongside Isaac Chiumbu as a Healing Apostle, a testament to his extraordinary abilities. Masedza's ministry took him to various locations, including Hwedza, Domboshava, and Bindura, where he preached with passion and authority, leaving a trail of transformed lives in his wake.

At this time, in the early 1930s, individuals like Langton Kupara, who would later become the first black superintendent of AFM in Zimbabwe in 1983, were not yet even members of AFM.

Krugar was well known because he went in the rural areas physically counting the adherents in a censors preceding the application to register the church. Corruption was not yet there in church circles, so Louis L. Kruger went around counting people, unlike the church people of today who play around with figures on the so called ghost people or workers.

On 30 November 1933, the Hwedza Native Commissioner complained that Louis L. Kruger was allowing black people to go around the rural areas preaching, unaccompanied by their white bosses. The commissioner had required Masedza to be under the supervision of a white man.

And so Masedza was disallowed to preach by the white government of the day. Louis L. Kruger and others complied because they were foreigners and back in South Africa there was more or less the same scenario. The Commissioner was incited by the complains of the mainline churches, particularly the Methodist church who had witnessed whole assemblies, pastors included, leaving to join AFM of South Africa. This methodist immigration to AFM continued even to the early 1950s, when my father, his pastor and the whole church joined AFM following my father who had courted the daughter of an AFM evangelist. The whole church crossing the floor for such a seemingly small thing, but God works in mysterious ways.

On the other hand, the authorities' concern were genuine. In its early days, the Apostolic Faith Mission (AFM) of South Africa in Zimbabwe was still in a relatively unstructured and primitive stage, lacking the formal organization and hierarchy of more established churches. However, despite this, the Holy Spirit's presence and power attracted numerous individuals from well-structured churches, leading to a significant influx of new members.

Ironically, today's AFM in Zimbabwe often expresses concerns when newer, unstructured churches woo people away from their congregations. This phenomenon is reminiscent of the early days of the AFM, when its founders, including charismatic leaders like John G. Lake and Louis Krugar, led exoduses from mainline churches to the AFM. These early leaders were instrumental in drawing people to the AFM's vibrant, Spirit-filled services, often at the expense of more traditional churches. It seems that the AFM in Zimbabwe has forgotten its own history, where it was once the beneficiary of people seeking a more dynamic, Pentecostal experience. Now, as more unstructured churches emerge, the AFM finds itself in a similar position as the traditional churches of the past, facing the challenge of retaining its members amidst the allure of newer, more flexible expressions of Christianity. This highlights the ongoing dynamic of spiritual seeking and the evolving landscape of religious affiliation in Zimbabwe.

In the early days of the Apostolic Faith Mission (AFM) in Zimbabwe, preachers donned dust coats while preaching, symbolizing humility and simplicity. Adherents were also discouraged from listening to radio broadcasts, deemed worldly and distracting from spiritual pursuits. Furthermore, the consumption of Coca-Cola was prohibited, as it was believed to contain cocaine or caffeine, considered harmful substances.

While some of these regulations may seem extreme by today's standards, they resonated with the church members of the time, who sought a more austere and dedicated spiritual life. Interestingly, one of the wealthiest individuals in the 2020s recently commented that Coca-Cola no longer contains cocaine, highlighting the evolution of societal norms and scientific understanding.

This phenomenon mirrored the experiences of its South African counterpart, the Apostolic Faith Mission (AFM) of South Africa in Natal, where the esteemed evangelist, Rev. Richard Ngidi, initially became affiliated with the AFM of South Africa. At that time, the AFM of South Africa exhibited strong Zionist tendencies, characterized by informal and unstructured meetings, as well as customs and practices drawn from the Old Testament. The liturgy, though unconventional and unappealing to mainline churches, proved remarkably effective in attracting large numbers of followers.

Notably, these Zionist tendencies were not unique to the Natal chapter but were, in fact, a pervasive feature of the black section of the AFM across various regions. Many assemblies within the AFM's black constituency exhibited similar characteristics, reflecting a distinct expression of faith that blended elements of African culture and tradition with Christian teachings. This distinctive approach to worship and practice resonated deeply with many blacks in the region, who found in it a sense of spiritual authenticity and connection to their heritage. As a result, the AFM's black section experienced significant growth and popularity, despite its divergence from more formalized and traditional Christian liturgies.

It is essential to acknowledge that the whites-only section of the Apostolic Faith Mission (AFM) church, although comprised of some individuals holding apartheid beliefs, largely suppressed the Zionistic teachings of John Lake and the movement of the Holy Spirit. This suppression stemmed from a desire to avoid drawing unwanted attention from the apartheid government, which might have viewed such practices as subversive or threatening to the status quo. Similarly, in Zimbabwe, the white-dominated church leadership also downplayed these teachings to maintain a safe distance from the authorities.

In stark contrast, Rev. William Duma's services at the Baptist Church in Lamontville attracted a diverse crowd, including white people and Indians, who would gather to hear him preach. Notably, during these services, attendees of all races would participate equally, without the usual segregationist norms prevailing at the time. This was a rare occurrence, as it was uncommon for white individuals to attend services led by a black pastor without white supervision. However, some courageous individuals defied this norm, recognizing the authenticity and power of Rev. Duma's ministry.

Rev. William Duma, an uneducated black man who spoke "broken" English, played a remarkable role as one of Rev. Richard Ngidi's mentors, guiding the educated Rev. Ngidi in his spiritual journey. This paradoxical relationship, where an uneducated individual mentored someone with formal education, exemplifies the mysterious and often unconventional ways of God. It highlights that spiritual wisdom and leadership are not solely dependent on human qualifications or credentials, but rather on the divine calling and anointing of God. As the Bible says, "God's ways are not our ways, and His thoughts are not our thoughts" (Isaiah 55:8). This remarkable mentorship serves as a testament to God's ability to use unexpected individuals to achieve His purposes.

This phenomenon speaks to the human tendency to prioritize conformity and self-preservation over spiritual conviction and truth. The Book of Revelation's mention of the "fearful" as the first group excluded from entering New Jerusalem (Revelation 21:8) serves as a poignant reminder of the consequences of allowing fear and complacency to dictate our actions, rather than embracing the transformative power of the Holy Spirit and the teachings of Christ.

However, as the Zimbabwean chapter of the Apostolic Faith Mission (AFM) of South Africa church grew, and supposedly more enlightened pastors took the helm, these Zionist and other teachings and practices gradually fell by the wayside. Unfortunately, the charismatic character and spiritual fervor that once defined the church also waned with the rise of these new leaders. The shift was largely driven by pressure from mainline churches and the government, which criticized the AFM's perceived excesses and lack of theological rigor. In response, the enlightened pastors sought to balance doctrine and practice, leading to a more formalized and institutionalized church, but one that may have lost some of its original spiritual intensity and distinctiveness.

And so, the preference for learned leaders over spirit-filled, shallowly educated ones has a long history in the church, dating back to the days of Wisdom, affectionately known as "madzibaba". This term was later adopted by the followers of Shonhihwa Masedza, also known as Johanne Masowe, who broke away to form the "Johane Masowe Chishanhu" church. Interestingly, members of this church address each other in the plural form, as "men" (madzibaba).

In 1938, W. Wilson, a key figure in the Apostolic Faith Mission (AFM), was struggling to establish a school in the colony. He wrote to authorities, expressing concerns about the replacement of European overseers with better-qualified individuals. In a subsequent letter, Wilson informed the government that unqualified European Overseers were being transferred from Rhodesia by the AFM Headquarters in Johannesburg. This may have included Louis L. Kruger, who disappears from records after 1938.

Ten years later, in 1948, Willard Wilson finally succeeded in opening a school at the AFM's newly purchased farm in Rufaro, offering classes up to standard three. Notably, Mrs. Wilson was among the teachers. Following his appointment as the leader of the AFM in 1953, W.L. Wilson oversaw significant developments, including the construction of a prestigious church building in Highfield. His leadership culminated in his appointment as Missionary Secretary in December 1954.

Let's retake the story of Wilson slowly. The renowned missionary Willard Wilson, affectionately known as Madzibaba, had arrived in Zimbabwe in the late 1930s, marking the beginning of a new era in the country's spiritual landscape. Shortly after, his brother joined him, bringing with him the necessary resources to establish another school in addition to the existing one at Gobatema. Willard Wilson is revered as the father of order, restoration, doctrine, and institutionalization within the Apostolic Faith Mission (AFM). He played a pivotal role in structuring the church, introducing a dress code for congregants, emphasizing hygiene practices, and establishing a sense of discipline and organization.

One of Wilson's most notable achievements was the procurement of Rufaro farm, which he initiated in 1943 and finally purchased in 1948. On this land, he built a school, but unfortunately, his vision for a Bible College never materialized. However, this idea was later realized by Rev. Cooks, who left for Zambia and founded Kasupe Bible College for AFM.

The first conference at Rufaro took place in 1952, marking a significant milestone in the church's history. Prior to this, conferences had been held in Gobatema and Gwanda since the 1920s. However, from 1949 to 1951, the conferences were temporarily relocated to Mupandawana in Gutu due to the lack of adequate ablution facilities at Rufaro. Wilson's leadership and vision laid the foundation for the growth and development of AFM in Zimbabwe, and his legacy continues to inspire and influence the church to this day.

The acquisition of Rufaro farm is steeped in prophetic significance, with Jahan Gwanzura (Chihari) reportedly foreseeing its purchase while at Gobatema, Gwanda, in the mid-1930s. According to accounts, Gwanzura proclaimed that God had promised to bestow upon the Apostolic Faith Mission (AFM) a conference center east of Gwanda, accompanied by a divine sign: rain or rainy clouds would manifest each time the faithful gathered at Rufaro. Remarkably, this phenomenon is believed to have occurred consistently since 1952, when the first conference was held at the newly acquired site.

However, the prophecy was met with a mixed response, with some residents of Matabeleland South expressing skepticism and suggesting that the Shona people were attempting to relocate the national center to their own territory. While the authenticity of the prophecy cannot be definitively confirmed or disputed, the reality remains that Rufaro was indeed purchased and has since become the site of annual conferences, starting in 1952 and continuing to this day.

It is worth noting that the fulfillment of this prophecy has been seen as a testament to God's faithfulness and provision for the AFM. The consistent manifestation of rain or rainy clouds at Rufaro conferences has become a cherished tradition, symbolizing the presence and blessing of God upon the gatherings. As the AFM continues to hold conferences at Rufaro, this phenomenon remains a powerful reminder of the prophetic roots and divine guidance that have shaped the church's history.

During the 1953/1954 season, a significant event took place at Rufaro, marking an important milestone in the lives of several influential figures in Zimbabwe's religious landscape. Notably, Ezekiel Handinawangu Guti, the founder of the Zimbabwe Assembly of God Assemblies (ZAOGA), and Langton Kupara, the first superintendent of the Apostolic Faith Mission (AFM) in Zimbabwe, were among those ordained as deacons at Rufaro. This ceremony was a pivotal moment in their spiritual journeys, occurring before they proceeded to further their theological education at Bible College.

This ordination ceremony marked a significant investment in the spiritual growth and development of these individuals, who would go on to play crucial roles in shaping the religious landscape of Zimbabwe. The fact that they were ordained as deacons at Rufaro, a site already steeped in prophetic significance, adds another layer of depth to their stories and ministries.

My maternal grandparents, uncle, and mother were all in attendance at this significant ordination ceremony. Notably, my father had not yet made the transition from the Methodist church to the Apostolic Faith Mission (AFM) at that time.

CHAPTER six

Navigating Politics and Faith: The Enduring Legacy of Enoch Gwanzura

The Gwanzura brothers, sons of Gwanzura Bonde, a prominent figure from Zvimba, and one of his eight wives, grew up in a vibrant and dynamic household with over forty half-siblings. After completing their education, the brothers ventured to Rimuka, Kadoma, where they established a thriving cobblers' shop and a popular restaurant in town. Their lives took a dramatic turn with the arrival of missionary S. Harris and his co-worker, Isaac Chiumbu, who introduced them to the Pentecostal faith. One day, Isaac Chiumbu, accompanied by Paul Karemba, visited the Gwanzura brothers' shoe-making shop to have his shoe repaired. Seizing the opportunity, they shared the Pentecostal gospel with the brothers, who eagerly embraced the message. This encounter led to a profound moment of meditation and silence, followed by a sudden outburst of speaking in tongues, uniting all six men in a powerful worship experience. From that transformative hour, Enoch Gwanzura and his brothers dedicated their lives to the Pentecostal faith, never looking back. This pivotal event marked the beginning of their spiritual journey, which would later influence their leadership roles in the Apostolic Faith Mission (AFM) and shape the course of Zimbabwe's religious history.

Let's delve into the fascinating story, specifically of Enoch Gwanzura, a pivotal figure in the administrative and political landscape of the Zimbabwean chapter of the Apostolic Faith Mission of South Africa. Enoch, along with his siblings, played a vital role in the church's advancement in Zimbabwe. Their journey began with a transformative experience at Gobatema, where they underwent orientation and immersed themselves in the local culture. During their time at Gobatema, they acquired the ability to speak Ndebele, a skill that may have been facilitated by the Holy Spirit or their own dedication to learning.

Enoch Gwanzura conducted clandestine nighttime worship meetings, a practice reminiscent of Zionist movements, echoing the methods of John Graham Lake, whose teachings had been instilled in him by his mentor, Isaac

Chiumbu. However, this secretive approach to worship did not sit well with the current leadership and government authorities, who viewed it with suspicion and concern.

Notably, Enoch's influence extended to the younger generation, including his future colleague, Jenias Chikwinya, who was just 10-15 years old when the Gwanzura siblings were at Gobatema for seminars. Enoch's own spiritual journey was marked by a significant transition, as he was baptized by Isaac Chiumbu after leaving the Methodist church. This experience ignited a passion within him, and he became a fiery lay preacher in his home area, spreading the message of the Apostolic Faith Mission with unbridled enthusiasm. He was nicknamed "vaDhotoronhomhi", because most of his sermons were from Deuteronomy.

In an effort to regain recognition, the Apostolic Faith Mission (AFM) in Johannesburg drafted new guidelines in 1935, which were more liberal and conciliatory towards the government and established missions. However, these efforts were met with resistance from Enoch Gwanzura, who vehemently opposed Rev. J. Wright, the representative from AFM Headquarters, at a meeting held at Gobatema farm in August 1935. The meeting, presided over by L. Kruger, had an undisclosed attendee, N.C. Mayabo, who was later revealed to be a government agent, possibly a plainclothes policeman, a secret service operative, or a detective from the criminal investigation department, but whose true identity and affiliation were not apparent at the time.

Enoch Gwanzura, who was assisting Swanepoel at Gobatema, saw the government as an obstacle to the work of the Holy Spirit and treated its authority with contempt. He was willing to face imprisonment for the sake of expanding the gospel. Unbeknownst to the attendees, the presence of the plainclothes policeman would ultimately cost them their provisional government recognition in 1936.

The situation escalated due to the failed agenda, culminating in a heated argument between Enoch Gwanzura and Rev. J. Wright, the representative from AFM Headquarters, at a meeting attended by government agent N.C. Mayabo.

Due to the lack of official recognition, missionaries were barred from entering native reserves, hindering their ability to reach local communities. The meeting, which had significant consequences for the mission, was attended by a group of key individuals, including Harris from Kadoma, Cusher from Umtali, Swanepoel from Gobatema, Isaac Kachadi (popularly known as Kadhi), and several others. Notably, Isaac Kachadi, also known as Kadhi, was a distinct individual who succeeded Isaac Chiumbu at the Kadoma native church, although Chiumbu was later attributed with the middle name Kachadi.

Then, in pursuit of official recognition, the Apostolic Faith Mission (AFM) in Johannesburg endeavored to enhance the caliber of their missionaries in Rhodesia. To achieve this, they strategically deployed educated, and experienced personnel: F.D. Johnston was stationed in Salisbury, O.P. Teichert (affectionately known as "Tiger") was assigned to Kadoma, and Wilson was placed in Gobatema. This deliberate move aimed to strengthen the mission's presence and credibility in the region.

At Gobatema, under Wilson's leadership, a deliberate effort was made to revamp the leadership structure by introducing more educated individuals from South Africa and the United States. This strategic move aimed to address the government's concerns about the educational background of existing leaders, thereby enhancing the mission's credibility and reputation.

However, Enoch Gwanzura, who lacked the desired level of education and had differing political views, was unable to adapt to this new framework. As a result, he relinquished his duties in Gobatema and established a new base of operations in the Zvimba reserve, where he could continue his work unfettered by the changing political and educational landscape.

Enoch Gwanzura became a self-appointed head minister and coordinator of AFM in the rural areas (reserves), while simultaneously extending the gospel to Harare, where he became associated with F. D. Johnstone.

Rev F.D. Johnston handled the situation with tact and sensitivity, aware of the simmering tensions within the black community, who felt increasingly marginalized from leadership roles. Rumors of potential splits within the church added to the delicate nature of the situation. Enoch Gwanzura, in particular, wielded significant influence, with a large following that trusted and believed in his leadership. Meanwhile, the church's head office in Johannesburg sought to maintain a policy of political neutrality, avoiding involvement in both ecclesiastical and national politics, especially as it pertained to their black constituents.

Under Enoch Gwanzura's leadership, three ministers, Yona Dingiswayo, Makobo Tshisenga, and Timothy Kadema, played key roles, while his brother, Johan Gwanzura, and Samson Gutsa, served as senior evangelists, alongside other educated evangelists who acted as Area ministers. This team of dedicated ministers worked together to advance the mission, with the Gwanzura brothers bringing their educational expertise to support the efforts of the entire team. Together, they supervised a team of evangelists with varying levels of education, including those with limited formal education and others with no formal education. Some notable examples of these evangelists include Zacharia Mugodi, Gabriel Chipoyera, Amon Nyika, James Ndebele, Simon Vambe, and Jenias Mufambi Chikwinya, among others. Within this group of evangelists, some had received formal education, but they faced challenges and disagreements with the leadership of the Apostolic Faith Mission. Despite their educational background, they encountered difficulties in their relationships with the mission's leaders.

Jenias Mufambi Chikwinya and his colleagues had even lower educational qualifications, yet they continued to serve in their pastoral roles under the supervision of more educated ministers, who themselves were not ordained as pastors. Only a select few of these native pastors were afforded the opportunity to attend Kasupe Bible College in Zambia for formal training in theological studies. Conversely, those who did not receive this training were gradually phased out of their roles, despite their congregations continuing to refer to them as pastors until their eventual retirement, either voluntarily or involuntarily.

Church historians in the Apostolic Faith Mission, specifically in Zimbabwe, tend to focus on a select few individuals, such as the Gwanzura brothers, as the primary evangelizers of Zimbabwe. However, numerous other dedicated ministers played a crucial role in the growth of the Apostolic Faith Mission of South Africa within Zimbabwe.

One such unsung hero is James Ndebele, who tirelessly served the Midlands region from the 1930s to the 1970s. Born around 1905, James Ndebele recalled that the Apostolic Faith Mission was already established in and around Gweru, particularly in the Chiundura reserve, by the time he was ten years old. He dedicated my mother to the Lord in 1934, when she was just two weeks old, and later dedicated my younger brother, Cosamu Ndhlovu, in 1965 in Kadoma.

Unfortunately, ministers like James Ndebele and Jenias Mufambi Chikwinya, who worked alongside the Gwanzura brothers, including Johan Gwanzura, are often overlooked in local AFM history. This may be due to their advanced age or limited literacy, which prevented them from attending Kasupe Bible College in Zambia. Despite this, their contributions to the spread of the Apostolic Faith Mission in Zimbabwe are invaluable and deserving of recognition.

Back to the story of Enoch Gwanzura, at the time when AFM Headquarters seconded F.D. Johnston in Salisbury, O.P. Teichert in Kadoma and Wilson in Gobatema, Enoch Gwanzura penetrated into Salisbury city.

It's noteworthy that the registration of the Apostolic Faith Mission (AFM) of South Africa in Zimbabwe was facilitated by a black man, Enoch Gwanzura, rather than a white missionary as initially intended. This development marked a significant turning point in the church's history.

Earlier, in April 1931, the Apostolic Faith Mission (AFM) had received conditional recognition for evangelistic purposes. However, in June 1932, the application submitted by Kruger and Harris for recognition as Missionary Superintendents was rejected. As a result, the AFM was unable to establish schools. Furthermore, the Gobatema School, which had previously been opened, was forced to close due to the missionaries' lack of adequate educational qualifications, as noted by the Inspector of the Native Development Department on June 22, 1932.

The recognition was short-lived, as the registration was withdrawn by 1934 due to various irregularities, as cited by the government at the time.

The church's official status was eventually restored through state registration in 1943, under the leadership of Enoch Gwanzura. Interestingly, this coincided with a significant breakaway from the white-led church, led by Isaac Chiumbu, who departed with over eighty percent of the total AFM membership, forming the African Apostolic Faith Mission (AAFM).

A controversial narrative surrounding Isaac Chiumbu has been widely circulated, alleging that he impregnated his wife's younger sister due to his wife's supposed barrenness. According to this account, Chiumbu was tried by a disciplinary panel and subsequently resigned from the Apostolic Faith Mission (AFM).

However, my grandfather vehemently disputes this story, highlighting Chiumbu's instrumental role in the church's expansion across Zimbabwe. In reality, Chiumbu faced unfair treatment and marginalization by white missionaries, who complied with the government's discriminatory policies. He was affectionately nicknamed "Kachembere" for his creative use of cookery illustrations during sermons.

Despite his dedication, Chiumbu was falsely accused of inappropriate behavior with women and denied a fair trial. In response, his supporters, comprising approximately 80% of the church's nationwide following, urged him to leave the white-controlled AFM and establish the African Apostolic Faith Mission, with its headquarters at Gadzema, near Chegutu. This pivotal event marked the most significant split in AFM history since 1908, driven by political rather than spiritual factors, and highlighted the ongoing struggle for equality and justice within the church.

While the motivations behind the government's decision to grant registration in 1943 are unclear, it's possible that it was, in part, a response to the significant loss of members and leadership the white-led AFM of South Africa had experienced due to the breakaway. Regardless, 1943 stands as a pivotal year in the history of both the AFM of South Africa's mission in Zimbabwe and the emergence of the African Apostolic Faith Mission (AAFM).

In a remarkable coincidence, on July 11 of the same year, 1943, Edna Gwanzura was born - a woman who would later make history in Zimbabwe's political landscape. She would go on to marry Forbes Madzongwe and become Ednah Madzongwe, a trailblazing female politician who served as the President of the Senate of the Republic of Zimbabwe from 2005 to 2018. Given her family's legacy, it's no surprise that Ednah pursued a career in politics. Her father, Enoch Gwanzura, was a prominent figure in the Apostolic Faith Mission (AFM) and a skilled politician in his own right, having navigated the complex political dynamics within the church. Enoch's political acumen and leadership skills likely influenced his children, with Ednah becoming a renowned politician, one of her sisters marrying a politician, and her brother serving as a senator under Ednah's presidency. This family's remarkable political legacy is a testament to the enduring impact of Enoch Gwanzura's leadership and vision.

Approximately four years after Rev F.D. Johnston had established a rapport with Enoch Gwanzura, a significant breakthrough occurred. The government's Secretary for Native Affairs, impressed by the progress made by the Apostolic Faith Mission of South Africa (AFM), submitted a favorable recommendation to the Minister of Native Affairs. This pivotal endorsement suggested considering the AFM for official recognition, thereby granting it equivalent facilities and privileges as other established denominations. Following a thorough review, the Minister of Native Affairs finally granted recognition and permission to the AFM on November 4, 1947. It is essential to note that registration and recognition are distinct processes; while registration merely records a church's existence, recognition confers official acknowledgment and accompanying benefits.

The Apostolic Faith Mission of South Africa's Zimbabwe mission field achieved a significant milestone in 1943 when Enoch Gwanzura successfully registered the church. Four years later, in 1947, missionary Rev F.D. Johnston submitted an application for recognition, which was ultimately granted, completing the church's accreditation by the government. This sequence of events reveals a poignant irony: despite the government's marginalization of blacks, the white-led church relied on the support and collaboration of black leaders like Enoch Gwanzura to gain acceptance and legitimacy. This dynamic underscores the complex power dynamics at play, where black voices were essential for the church's success, even as they faced systemic oppression.

The third coincidence: 1943 marked a significant year for the Apostolic Faith Mission (AFM) of South Africa, as it was the year that P. E. LeRoux retired from his 30-year tenure as president. Although his leadership played a crucial role in shaping the church's trajectory, the change in presidency may also have contributed to the successful registration of the AFM in Zimbabwe, paving the way for the church's growth and expansion in the region.

(When Johnston left he was replaced by C. du Plessis who took charge of Harare.)

As a skilled politician in his own right, and having navigated the complex political dynamics within the AFM, Enoch Sireu Gwanzura, son of Gwanzura Bonde's political acumen and leadership skills likely influenced the likes of Langton Kupara, who would be the first black superintendent of the Apostolic Faith Mission in Zimbabwe, after a clandestine demand of independence front the AFM of South Africa.

CHAPTER seven

The 1983 Turnaround: A New Era for AFM in Zimbabwe

In the initial months following the founding of the Apostolic Faith Mission (AFM) in 1908, the church practiced racial integration, with both white and non-white members being baptized together.

However, towards the end of 1908, Afrikaans-speaking brothers joined the Executive Council, bringing with them a deeper understanding of South Africa's complex racial dynamics. This led to a gradual separation of the races within the church.

Although the AFM began as a racially integrated body, the American missionaries eventually adopted prevailing social norms and divided the church into four main sections: black, mixed race, Indian, and white. This segregation was not driven by theological conviction, but rather by the societal pressures of the time.

It was only after the departure of the American missionaries that the AFM succumbed to racial segregation, deviating from its initial non-racial stance due to external pressures rather than internal beliefs.

Fast-forward to 1960, the year of the author's birth, when two pivotal events occurred in the Apostolic Faith Mission of South Africa (AFM) church. Firstly, the white section of the church underwent a transformation, effectively becoming an Afrikaans-dominated church that inadvertently supported the racist apartheid policies of the South African government. This shift led to further entrenchment of segregation within the church.

Concurrently, the Native Workers' Conference addressed a crucial motion, which was adopted in 1961. The motion established a clear distinction between two categories of workers within the black section of the AFM: 'Ministers' and 'Evangelists'. Ministers would possess specific powers, as outlined in their certificates, and lead congregations. Evangelists, while possessing the same powers, would not have a fixed congregation and would only administer the

Lord's Supper at the request of the minister in charge. This decision led to the formalization of titles for AFM workers, including Ministers (or Pastors), Evangelists, Elders, Deacons, and Deaconesses.

In 1969, Pastor E.J. Gschwend's assumption of leadership marked the dawn of a new era for the mixed-race section of the church. Under his guidance, the section transitioned from being controlled and managed by the Missions Department to being led and managed by its own Executive Council, comprised of mixed-race leaders. As the mixed-race work expanded across the country, new districts were established, leading to the appointment of additional missionaries as overseers to support the growing ministry.

The contributions of these additional missionaries played a significant role in the expansion of the mixed-race work. Through their dedication and hard work, new assemblies were established, and new church buildings were constructed, providing a physical presence for the growing community. Two notable leaders, Pastor D.W. Patrick and Pastor C.A. Botes, made substantial contributions during this period.

Pastor D.W. Patrick served as the vice chairperson of the mixed-race Workers' Council from 1969 until his retirement in 1977, providing leadership and guidance during a critical phase of growth. His commitment and expertise helped shape the council's decisions and actions, paving the way for further expansion.

Similarly, Pastor C.A. Botes served as the general secretary from 1969 until his retirement in 1982, playing a vital role in the administrative and organizational aspects of the mixed-race work. His tireless efforts ensured the smooth operation of the church's activities, enabling the community to flourish.

In 1983, the white section of the Apostolic Faith Mission (AFM) in South Africa took a significant step towards unity and equality by drafting a new constitution for all sections of the church. This move aimed to create a single, unified identity for the AFM, with a constitution that would apply to all sections, each with its own policy tailored to its specific needs. The new constitution ensured that any changes would require the consent of all sections and a two-thirds majority in each respective Workers' Council.

This development was likely influenced by the Zimbabwean church's demand for independence from the South African church, as well as the political climate in South Africa, where whites feared repercussions from non-white members amidst the country's growing nationalist movement.

In 1983, a significant milestone marked the transformation of the Apostolic Faith Mission (AFM) in Zimbabwe. Rev. Gashwend, the then Missions Director in the Apostolic Faith Mission of South Africa, officially handed over the reins of the church to Langton Kupara, signifying the complete transition of the AFM from a South African-led mission to a locally led church. This historic event gave birth to the AFM in Zimbabwe as a distinct entity, separate from the earlier Zimbabwean Mission of the AFM of South Africa, which had operated from 1915 to 1983 (a span of 68 years).

During the ceremony, Rev. Gashwend symbolically presented Langton Kupara with a golden watch, commemorating the transfer of leadership and the dawn of a new era for the AFM in Zimbabwe. This gesture marked the culmination of a long process, as the church transitioned from foreign leadership to local stewardship, paving the way for a more indigenous and self-sustaining ministry. The year 1983 thus represents the official birthdate of the AFM in Zimbabwe, a milestone that would shape the church's future growth and development.

The Apostolic Faith Mission (AFM) in Zimbabwe's Hymn Book bears the distinctive signature of Rev. Langton Kupara, the pioneering National Leader of AFM in Zimbabwe. This significant detail serves as a testament to the fact that AFM in Zimbabwe was formally established in 1983 as an autonomous entity, emerging from the Apostolic Faith Mission of South Africa. Rev. Kupara's signature on the Hymn Book symbolizes his instrumental role in leading the church's transition from a South African-led mission to a self-governing body, marking a new chapter in the history of AFM in Zimbabwe.

The Apostolic Faith Mission (AFM) in Zimbabwe is affiliated with AFM International; therefore, its global history indeed traces back to May 25, 1908. The Southern Rhodesia chapter, now Zimbabwe, officially began in 1915 as part of the AFM of South Africa, although migrant natives had introduced the church as early as December 1908.

However, it's important to note that the AFM in Zimbabwe is no longer a subsidiary of the AFM of South Africa, as it was from 1908 to 1983. Instead, it has become an autonomous entity within the AFM International network, with its own distinct identity and history, which commenced with the handover of leadership to Langton Kupara in 1983. This marks a significant distinction between the church's global heritage and its local evolution.

The establishment of the Apostolic Faith Mission (AFM) in Zimbabwe was driven by several key factors. Primarily, the church was previously governed from outside its borders, limiting its ability to function autonomously and make decisions that best suited its local context. This external control was particularly problematic given Zimbabwe's recent fight for independence from racist and segregationist rule. Native leaders within the church sought to break free from oppressive leadership structures that perpetuated the same racist attitudes they had fought against in the political sphere.

As mentioned earlier, the Apostolic Faith Mission (AFM) of South Africa, like numerous other denominations, was a segregated society, reflecting the profound impact of South African politics on ecclesiastical politics during the apartheid era. The country's racist policies and laws, enforced from 1948 to 1994, permeated various aspects of society, including religious institutions. Consequently, the AFM of South Africa was characterized by racial divisions, with separate congregations and leadership structures for white and black members.

The Zimbabwean chapter of the AFM faced an even more complex and challenging situation. Not only was it influenced by the apartheid-era policies of its foreign-based leadership, but it was also shaped by the internal government of Rhodesia (now Zimbabwe), which had its own brand of discriminatory policies. During the Rhodesian era (1965-1979), the government enforced segregationist laws, restricting the rights and freedoms of black citizens. This toxic blend of external and internal influences exacerbated racial divisions within the Zimbabwean chapter of the AFM, making it even more entrenched than its South African counterpart.

The AFM's segregationist policies and practices during this period were a stark contradiction to the fundamental teachings of Christianity, which emphasize unity, equality, and love among all believers. The legacy of this painful era continues to impact the church's efforts towards reconciliation, healing, and true unity in diversity.

Many individuals who had previously broken away from the AFM of South Africa to form their own denominations did so to escape the oppressive regime of the government and white church leadership. However, the black church leaders who sought to establish an independent AFM in Zimbabwe proceeded with caution, careful not to be perceived as rebelling against their white counterparts. Instead, they strategically maneuvered to assume leadership roles without openly challenging the existing power structure.

This quiet transfer of power parallels the events of 2017 in Zimbabwe (34 years later), where a military-assisted transition, dubbed "Operation Restore Legacy," took place. This transition was described by some as a "coup that is not a coup," highlighting the subtle and nuanced nature of the power shift. Similarly, the black leadership of the AFM of South Africa's Zimbabwe chapter clandestinely assumed control, with many members unaware of the details surrounding the transition.

In this context, the Apostolic Faith Mission in Zimbabwe emerged as a distinct entity from the Apostolic Faith Mission of South Africa, marking a significant milestone in the church's history and its journey towards autonomy and self-determination.

The Zionist church in South Africa, established before the arrival of the Apostolic Faith Mission (AFM) in 1908, experienced a similar trajectory. Initially, the Zionist church was led by white revivalists, but most of its black members eventually joined the AFM. However, when conflicts arose, senior black leaders, Lekganyane and Samuel Moyo, broke away from the AFM to form separate factions of the original Zionist church. Lekganyane founded the Zion Christian Church of Mount Morija in Petersburg, while Samuel Moyo established the Zion Christian Church, which is now predominantly Zimbabwean.

The motivations behind Lekganyane and Moyo's initial joining of the AFM are unclear. It is possible that they genuinely sought to be part of the AFM, or that they had a hidden agenda to eventually establish their own denominations, thereby supplanting the original white Zionist church. Regardless of their intentions, it is evident that they strategically planned their departure from the AFM, paving the way for the successful establishment of their respective churches.

Both the Zion Christian Church of Mount Morija and the Zion Christian Church founded by Samuel Moyo have continued to thrive to this day, demonstrating the resilience and determination of their founders. This phenomenon highlights the complex dynamics of church politics and they stayed in their often-blurred lines between cooperation and competition within religious movements.

CHAPTER eight

Delayed Autonomy: Navigating Church Politics and Social Change

The delayed assumption of local leadership by black leaders within the Apostolic Faith Mission (AFM) in Zimbabwe, until 1983, two and a half years after the country's independence in 1980, raises important questions. Despite years of political instability, racial segregation, and oppressive laws, some black leaders remained loyal to the AFM of South Africa, seemingly acquiescing to the prevailing segregation norms. This loyalty is puzzling, especially when contrasted with the bold actions of leaders like Shonhiwa Masedza and Isaac Chiumbu, who broke away to form their own denominations and thrived despite the oppressive environment.

The silence of AFM of South Africa leaders during this period is striking, particularly given the flourishing of breakaway churches. Was their inaction driven by fear of repression, or were other factors at play? It appears that the AFM of South Africa leadership only became interested in establishing an independent church in Zimbabwe after the country's political landscape had changed. This raises questions about their motivations and commitment to empowering local leadership during the tumultuous years of segregation and oppression.

The delayed transition to local leadership also highlights the complex dynamics of church politics during times of social change. The AFM of South Africa's delayed response may have been influenced by a range of factors, including internal power struggles, fear of losing control, or a lack of understanding of the local context. Regardless, the belated assumption of local leadership by black Zimbabweans marked a significant turning point in the country's ecclesiastical history, paving the way for greater autonomy and self-determination within the church.

This phenomenon was not unique to Zimbabwe; similar dynamics played out in South Africa as well. While some leaders broke away to form their own independent denominations, others chose to remain within the segregated church structure, yet continued to work towards change from within. Despite the oppressive nature of the segregational system, these individuals demonstrated remarkable humility and perseverance, opting to strive for reform and equality within the existing framework rather than abandoning it altogether. Their decision to stay and work towards transformation from within reflects a complex and nuanced approach to addressing the injustices of the time.

For example, as mentioned earlier, during the colonial era, the influence of politics inevitably seeped into ecclesiastical politics, threatening to disrupt the unity and harmony of the church. However, visionary leaders like Rev. Richard Ngidi of South Africa and his predecessor, Rev. Elias Letwaba, wisely recognized the potential dangers of entangling politics with spiritual matters. They understood that allowing political discussions to dominate church meetings would not only hurt congregants but also create tension and division, particularly between black members and white missionaries.

Rev. Elias Letwaba, one of the pioneering black leaders of the Apostolic Faith Mission (AFM), had already set a powerful example by establishing a thriving African church in northern South Africa despite facing racial indignities and discrimination from white church leaders. Yet, he remained silent on political matters, choosing instead to focus on spreading the Gospel and building a united church.

Similarly, Rev. Richard Ngidi (1921-1985), followed in Elias Letwaba's footsteps, deliberately avoiding political discussions in the meetings he attended. With a heart full of love and compassion, Ngidi sought to create a safe and inclusive space for all congregants, regardless of their racial or social background. His leadership was marked by humility, wisdom, and a commitment to transcending the racial and social divisions that threatened to fragment the church. By keeping the focus on spiritual growth and unity, Ngidi and leaders like him helped to build a strong, resilient church that could weather the storms of political turmoil and social change.

Let's take a brief look at Letwaba's life and ministry before we dive deeper.

Elias Letwaba was born in 1870 in Middelburg, Transvaal. He was well-educated, fluent in seven languages, and preached with his brother Wilfred from a young age.

At 39 years old, he was baptized in the Zion Apostolic Church.

In April 1908, he met John G. Lake and Tom Hezmalhalch at the Zulu Mission. Letwaba was invited to the pulpit to stand alongside Lake, which angered some white colonialists, but Lake stood his ground and even kissed Letwaba.

Elias Letwaba became a key figure in the Apostolic Faith Mission, supervising native churches and opening the Patmos Bible School in 1924. He preached fervently, leading services in six churches on Sundays and teaching at the Bible school during the week.

Letwaba witnessed over 10,000 healings in his lifetime and is said to have received the mantle of Lake's healing ministry in South Africa. He retired from teaching at 65 and died in 1959 at the age of 89.

Let's look into the following three generations. Elias Letwaba (1870-1959), was fifty-one years older than Richard Ngidi (1921-1985), and Letwaba worked alongside John Lake (1870-1935), who was the same age with him, though Lake died twenty-four years earlier. Now, in come Frank Chikane (born 1951), who is therty years younger than Richard Ngidi.

(On a fascinating note, have you noticed the remarkable coincidence that three influential figures in the same spiritual lineage share the same birth year? William Seymour, who mentored John Lake, John Lake, who mentored Elias Letwaba, and Elias Letwaba, who founded Patmos Bible College to mentor future generations, were all born in 1870. This striking synchronicity reminds us that with God, nothing occurs by chance; everything is part of a larger, divine plan.)

In this set up, both John Lake and Elias Letwaba are in the first generation of the Apostolic Faith Mission of South Africa, Richard Ngidi in the second generation, and Frank Chikane in the third.

Rev. Chikane is a remarkable example of the third generation of black Pentecostal leaders in the Apostolic Faith Mission (AFM) of South Africa.

Born in 1951 and raised in the urban high-density suburb of Soweto, Johannesburg, Chikane's leadership style and approach differ significantly from those of his predecessors, such as Elias Letwaba and Richard Ngidi. Unlike the earlier generations of leaders, who focused primarily on spiritual salvation, healing, and deliverance, Chikane's ministry was shaped by the harsh economic and social realities of his time.

Growing up in Soweto during the apartheid era, Chikane witnessed firsthand the struggles of his community, including poverty, inequality, and social injustice. As a result, he became a strong advocate for social and economic transformation, believing that Christian meekness should not be equated with weakness. Chikane's leadership emphasized the need for holistic healing, addressing both spiritual and material needs, and challenging the status quo.

In contrast to the more conservative approach of some pastors in the 1960s and 1970s, Chikane was a vocal critic of apartheid and an active participant in the fight against social injustice. His leadership style was characterized by a strong sense of social responsibility, and he worked tirelessly to empower his community through education, economic development, and social activism.

Through his ministry, Chikane demonstrated that faith and activism are not mutually exclusive, but rather complementary aspects of a holistic approach to Christianity. His legacy continues to inspire a new generation of leaders in the AFM and beyond, who seek to address the complex social and economic challenges facing their communities.

After receiving his Diploma in Theology in 1979, Frank Chikane was ordained as an AFM pastor in March 1980, the same year he married Kagiso. However, in August 1981, he was suspended by the West Rand District Council for remaining active in politics, despite promising to abstain during his ordination. His one-year suspension ended in October 1982, but he never received formal reinstatement, only a request to return his credentials. Undeterred, Chikane remained a church member while pursuing high-profile politics, closely watched by black congregants and the revolutionary-minded Zimbabwean pastorate.

Fortunately, Rev. Edgar Gschwend was there to support him and others in similar situations, be it directly or indirectly. Gschwend was a man who tirelessly worked to create a level playing field for all workers in the Missions he directed. Thankfully, he served as Missions Director at a crucial time, not only for South Africa and Zimbabwe but perhaps globally, making a significant impact on the lives of many.

Emboldened by the pioneering spirit of Enoch Gwanzura, inspired by revolutionary leaders like Pastor Frank Chikane, and galvanized by the dawn of independence in Zimbabwe, the black leaders of the Apostolic Faith Mission (AFM) in Zimbabwe found the courage to demand autonomy from the South African church. This bold move was further energized by the guidance of Missions Director Edgar Gschwend, whose tireless efforts had fostered a sense of unity and purpose among the native congregations.

As Zimbabwe shed the shackles of colonial rule, the AFM leaders in the country began to envision a similar liberation from the administrative control of their South African counterparts. They sought to establish a distinct identity, tailored to the unique needs and context of the Zimbabwean people. This desire for self-determination was rooted in a deep-seated conviction that the church should be led by those who intimately understood the local culture, challenges, and aspirations.

With Gschwend's support, the black leaders of the AFM in Zimbabwe rallied together, drawing strength from their shared experiences and collective wisdom. They presented a united front, advocating for independence and the opportunity to chart their own course. This courageous stance marked a significant turning point in the history of the AFM in Zimbabwe, as they embarked on a journey towards self-governance and contextualized ministry.

Rev. Edgar Gschwend, born on August 21, 1929, in Lesotho, was a third-generation leader with a rich missionary heritage. As the son and grandson of missionaries, he was uniquely equipped to lead the Apostolic Faith Mission (AFM) in South Africa. Ordained by the AFM in June 1953, Gschwend embarked on missionary work, demonstrating his dedication to spreading the gospel.

Gschwend's leadership trajectory within the AFM was marked by significant milestones. In 1969, he became the assistant to the Missions Superintendent, and two years later, in 1971, he assumed the role of Superintendent, overseeing the missions department. His collaboration with renowned evangelist Reinhard Bonnke in the evangelistic association yielded remarkable numerical growth for the AFM.

Gschwend's impact extended beyond evangelism, as he tirelessly worked to address and dissolve racial tensions and problems that had developed within the AFM over the years. His commitment to unity and reconciliation was evident in his leadership.

In addition to his missions work, Gschwend served as the second principal of the Bible School at Lady Selborne, near Pretoria, from 1953 to 1955. He trained all-black workers, laying a foundation for future leaders. After resigning, he founded "All Nations," a literature distribution organization that spread gospel messages across the continent.

One of his notable publications, "The Human Heart Book" (Mwoyo Womunhu), became popular in Zimbabwe. This booklet poignantly illustrated the contrasts between a righteous and unrighteous heart, leaving a lasting impact on readers.

As Missions Director, Rev. Edgar Gschwend stands out as one of the most effective leaders in the history of the Apostolic Faith Mission, leaving an indelible mark on the church's growth, unity, and evangelistic endeavors.

While the Apostolic Faith Mission (AFM) of South Africa's Zimbabwe chapter may have drawn inspiration from third-generation pastors like Frank Chikane, who played a significant role in shaping the church's trajectory, there are a couple of unfavorable things that the revolutionary mentality activated in the church. Those who recall the 1970s and earlier years often note that while the AFM in Zimbabwe has grown exponentially in numbers and infrastructure since 1983, surpassing its predecessor, the spiritual fervor and momentum of the past have yet to be matched by the contemporary church.

This phenomenon raises important questions about the dynamics of spiritual movements and the challenges of sustaining momentum across generations. Despite the AFM's impressive growth and expansion, the earlier years were marked by a unique intensity and passion that has yet to be replicated. This disparity highlights the need for continuous spiritual renewal and revival to ensure that the church remains vibrant and effective in its mission.

Some may argue that the demand for independence from the South African church was not driven by AFM leaders, but rather by the newly formed government of Zimbabwe, which warned that it would phase out all foreign-controlled organizations, particularly those from South Africa, due to the ongoing apartheid regime. However, this raises questions about what the Apostolic Faith Mission of South Africa would gain from granting independence to its Zimbabwean chapter. In reality, it was the Zimbabwean church that stood to benefit, as all AFM properties in Zimbabwe had title deeds belonging to the South African church. This likely motivated the sale of Gobatema Farm by the AFM of South Africa.

The Zimbabwean chapter's push for independence was a shrewd move, taking advantage of the country's newfound autonomy. Coaxing the church leadership in Johannesburg was easier due to the uncertainty surrounding the apartheid government at the time. Notably, the Missions Director officiated at the handover and takeover ceremony, despite the fact that the Church in Zimbabwe still belonged to the mother church in South Africa, with a president, secretary, and executive board that could have officially handed over the mission field to Zimbabweans.

Interestingly, the white members of the Apostolic Faith Mission of South Africa's Zimbabwe chapter simply vacated the premises, and today, any white person seen at the National Conference Center of the AFM in Zimbabwe is merely a visitor. Since the formation of the AFM in Zimbabwe in 1983, the country no longer has white members, marking a significant shift in the church's demographics.

It is striking that the Apostolic Faith Mission (AFM) in Zimbabwe, a church with millions of members locally and a global presence spanning five continents, has no local white families attending its national conferences at the Zimbabwe National Conference Center. Despite having 32 church provinces across the country's 10 political subdivisions, not a single white member serves on any assembly committee. This stark reality indicates a complete absence of white members within the AFM in Zimbabwe. Given this, it is ironic that the current church leadership could discuss the segregation prevalent during colonial times, when in fact, the church itself appears to have inadvertently perpetuated a similar separation along racial lines.

It is intriguing that the Apostolic Faith Mission in Zimbabwe is still colloquially known as "Krugar's Church" (Chechi yekwaKrugar), a nod to its growth and development under the influence of a white missionary, Louis L. Krugar. Ironically, the African Apostolic Faith Mission once referred to it as "The Whites' Church". This legacy raises questions about our collective past and whether it is something to be proud of. As we move forward, may God guide us towards a more inclusive future. Our aim should be to become a church that warmly welcomes people of all races in Zimbabwe, as well as international visitors, fostering a truly diverse and united community.

In the Zimbabwean government, we see a small but notable presence of white individuals, some of whom hold prominent positions as political councilors, members of parliament, and even ministers and deputy ministers. This begs the question: why is it that the Apostolic Faith Mission (AFM) in Zimbabwe, a church that values diversity and inclusivity, does not have a similar diversity?

In addition to the deeply ingrained and long-standing issue of silent racial discrimination, which must be addressed and rectified at all costs, even among pastoral leadership, the church, particularly Pentecostal denominations like the Apostolic Faith Mission (AFM), continues to struggle with another persistent problem: the divisive dynamics of seniority versus juniority, and wealth disparity. This ongoing issue creates a harmful dichotomy between those in positions of power and influence, and those who are less affluent or newer to the ministry, hindering the church's ability to function as a unified body.

A recurring issue within the Apostolic Faith Mission (AFM) head offices is the tendency to assign intens or inexperienced pastors to fledgling assemblies that lack established structures and support systems. These junior pastors are often sent to areas with minimal or no existing membership, expecting them to establish a thriving congregation from scratch. In some cases, they may be the only pastor, or even the sole believer, in the area. Despite these challenging circumstances, these dedicated pastors answer their calling by preaching with passion and conviction, often to a tiny audience, trusting in Jesus' promise to be present among even the smallest gatherings (Matthew 18:20).

Through their faithfulness and God's grace, these small assemblies gradually grow, and as they begin to flourish, particularly financially, a senior pastor is often assigned to take over. This approach highlights a concerning trend in the modern church, where the focus has shifted from evangelism and winning new souls to merely maintaining existing congregations. Unlike the AFM of old, which prioritized spreading the Gospel and growing the flock, today's church often seems more concerned with preserving the status quo and catering to the needs of established members rather than actively seeking new converts. This lack of emphasis on evangelism has resulted in a shortage of passionate evangelists and a surplus of pastors who primarily focus on shepherding and milking the existing flock.

This phenomenon is further exacerbated by the fact that many senior pastors are more focused on building their own legacies and empires within the church, rather than prioritizing the Great Commission. They often surround themselves with yes-men and create a culture of fear, where dissenting voices are silenced and true discipleship is hindered. As a result, the church becomes a mere shadow of its former self, with more emphasis on pomp and ceremony than on genuine spiritual growth and outreach. The consequences of this approach are far-reaching, leading to a stagnation of the church's impact and influence in the world.

The Great Commission's clarion call to "Go ye therefore..." resonates with every individual, but particularly with pastors who claim a divine calling to serve. However, as we assess the current state of the church, we must confront a sobering question: Is this still the authentic church founded by Christ Jesus through his faithful servants, or has it been compromised by human frailty and complacency? The harvest of our actions will be revealing - we shall reap what we have sown!

CHAPTER Nine

The Victors' Account: Unpacking the Biases and Omissions in AFM's Historical Record

"History is written by the victors" is a famous quote often attributed to Winston Churchill, although its origin is unclear. The phrase suggests that the winners of a conflict or struggle are the ones who get to shape the narrative of what happened, while the perspectives of the losers are often marginalized or suppressed.

This phrase highlights the idea that history is not always an objective or neutral account of events, but rather a subjective interpretation shaped by the interests and biases of those in power. The victors may downplay or omit their own mistakes and atrocities, while exaggerating the faults and weaknesses of their opponents.

This concept has been observed throughout history, where the dominant group or nation has controlled the narrative, often distorting or erasing the experiences and contributions of marginalized or defeated groups.

Throughout history, the adage "history is written by the victors" has held true in various contexts. In the era of colonialism, European powers imposed their dominance over indigenous cultures, and subsequently, they penned the narrative of their conquests. From their perspective, they were the harbingers of civilization, bringing light to the supposedly dark and savage lands they encountered. In stark contrast, the colonized peoples' stories, achievements, and experiences were often distorted, suppressed, or erased.

Similarly, the winners of wars have traditionally been the ones to chronicle the conflicts, casting themselves as heroic liberators and their vanquished foes as brutal aggressors. This skewed narrative has perpetuated a biased understanding of historical conflicts, neglecting the complexities and nuances of the events.

Furthermore, victorious political movements and ideologies have also been known to rewrite history to legitimize their actions and discredit their adversaries. By controlling the narrative, they have sought to justify their policies, ideologies, and decisions, often at the expense of marginalized or opposing voices. This phenomenon has contributed to a distorted understanding of historical events, underscoring the importance of seeking diverse perspectives and challenging dominant narratives.

However, it's essential to note that this phrase is not absolute, and there are many examples of alternative histories and counter-narratives that challenge the dominant perspective. Historians and scholars strive to present a more balanced and accurate account of events, incorporating diverse voices and perspectives.

Some proponents of biased history, which favors the powerful and victorious, are not even true victors but rather cunning individuals seeking prestige and self-aggrandizement. A striking example of this phenomenon can be seen in the rewritten history of Zimbabwe's earliest settlers. Certain individuals have manipulated historical records to prioritize their own totems and clans, despite the fact that ancient writings from Portuguese and Arab traders, who had extensive interactions with Zimbabwe, make no mention of these names.

These revisionists claim that their ancestors migrated from the Great Lakes region and other distant areas, yet historians and records from those regions contradict this narrative, revealing a glaring lack of evidence to support such claims. This blatant distortion of history serves only to perpetuate a false narrative, obscuring the true story of Zimbabwe's earliest settlers and reinforcing a skewed perspective that benefits only a select few.

I vividly recall the occasion when I was about to sit for my Grade Seven primary school examinations. As part of the registration process, I needed to produce a birth certificate. My parents, however, didn't have one readily available. Without hesitation, they visited the church registrar, who happened to be the evangelist or elder, at their home. They obtained a duplicate certificate of my baby dedication, which had taken place twelve years prior. With this document in hand, they proceeded to the Registrar of Births in Que-Que and submitted it as proof of my birth. Remarkably, the birth certificate was issued without any questions or complications.

This incident highlights the significant role the church played in our community as a reliable source of information and authentic record-keeper. The church's records were trusted and respected by government authorities, and its documentation was accepted as valid proof of important life events like birth. This level of trust and credibility is a testament to the church's influence and standing in our society at the time.

Fast-forward to the present day, and it's disheartening to note that the situation has changed dramatically. The church's records are no longer viewed with the same level of trust and authenticity. This decline in credibility is a cause for concern, and one can't help but wonder what factors have contributed to this shift. Has the church's role in the community diminished? Have its records become less reliable? Whatever the reasons, it's clear that the church's influence and standing have been eroded over time, and that's a sad state of affairs.

The church, as an institution, has strayed from its divine mandate to be "in the world but not of the world," just as its Lord and Savior Jesus Christ declared in John 17:11 and 16. Instead of maintaining its distinctiveness and holiness, the visible church has become increasingly entangled with the world's values, systems, and practices. This compromise has resulted in a loss of spiritual purity and authenticity, causing governments and other entities to view the church with skepticism and distrust.

The invisible church, comprising true believers who hold fast to their faith and values, remains untainted by the world's influences. However, the visible church, with its institutional structures and human leadership, has succumbed to worldly pressures and temptations. This has led to a blurring of lines between the sacred and the secular, causing the church to lose its prophetic voice and moral authority.

As a consequence, governments and other organizations no longer regard the church as a trusted partner or a beacon of truth and integrity. The church's involvement in worldly pursuits, such as politics, wealth, and power struggles, has tarnished its reputation and eroded its credibility. The world now views the church as just another institution, driven by self-interest and agendas, rather than a transformative force for spiritual renewal and social justice.

This state of affairs is a far cry from the church's original purpose and calling. The apostle Paul's admonition to the Colossian church to "set your minds on things above, not on earthly things" (Colossians 3:2) seems to have fallen on deaf ears. The church's failure to maintain its heavenly focus has resulted in a loss of spiritual power, relevance, and trust.

In this trend, the Apostolic Faith Mission (AFM) in Zimbabwe has not been immune to the phenomenon of rewriting history with a biased perspective, often prioritizing a particular narrative or agenda over factual accuracy. Like many institutions, the AFM has fallen prey to the temptation of presenting its past in a manner that serves the interests and agendas of those currently in power. This subjective interpretation of history is shaped by personal biases, leading to a deliberate omission of crucial events, figures, and contributions that have been instrumental in shaping the church's journey.

Regrettably, the AFM in Zimbabwe has chosen to sideline and marginalize some of its own pioneers and church elders who toiled tirelessly to establish and grow the church. These dedicated individuals, who played a vital role in laying the foundation for the church's current success, have been conveniently left out of the narrative. Their stories, experiences, and achievements have been ignored or downplayed, effectively erasing their contributions from the church's collective memory.

By rewriting its history in this manner, the AFM in Zimbabwe is, in fact, adopting the world's approach to recording the past. This approach prioritizes the interests of the powerful and neglects the voices and experiences of those who have been marginalized or overlooked. The church's history is thus reduced to a sanitized and incomplete account, lacking the richness and complexity that a more inclusive and honest narrative would provide.

This biased rewriting of history not only distorts the church's true heritage but also undermines the very principles of integrity, honesty, and transparency that the church is called to uphold. By ignoring the contributions of its own pioneers and elders, the AFM in Zimbabwe risks losing sight of its roots and the values that have sustained it thus far.

Historically, white missionaries played a significant role in shaping the narrative of events within the Apostolic Faith Mission (AFM), particularly when it came to the characters and actions of black church leaders. Their reports to the head office in Johannesburg often carried a biased tone, casting blame on the factions that chose to leave the church. This phenomenon perpetuated a skewed understanding of the breakaways and splits within the AFM, as the voices of those who departed were frequently silenced or ignored.

The adage "history is written by the victors" rings true in this context, as the dominant group's perspective was prioritized, while the experiences and contributions of marginalized individuals and groups were downplayed or omitted. The winners, often celebrated as heroes, had their stories told and retold, while the losers' voices faded into obscurity.

Fast-forward to 1983, when the AFM in Zimbabwe finally gained independence. One would expect a more balanced and inclusive narrative to emerge. However, the rewritten history of the AFM in Zimbabwe also exhibits biases and omissions. The accounts center around a select few families and individuals, neglecting the contributions and struggles of many others who were marginalized alongside them.

Notably, the existence of "whites-only" assemblies in Zimbabwe is barely acknowledged, with no examination of their impact or legacy. What role did these churches play in the broader context of the AFM? How did their actions influence the current state of the church? These questions remain unanswered, leaving a glaring gap in the historical record.

By neglecting to confront and include the complexities of their past, the AFM in Zimbabwe risks perpetuating a sanitized and incomplete narrative. It is essential to acknowledge and learn from the experiences of all individuals and groups, regardless of their race or status, to gain a more comprehensive understanding of the church's history and its ongoing legacy.

Unlike human organizations, including church denominations, the Bible is remarkable for its unflinching honesty and transparency. It presents individuals and events as they truly were, without glossing over flaws or imperfections. A prime example is the story of David, a man revered as being "after God's own heart" (1 Samuel 13:14, Acts 13:22). Despite his exemplary faith and leadership, the Bible candidly records his mistakes, including his infamous encounter with Bathsheba (2 Samuel 11) and his subsequent cover-up. This unvarnished portrayal is not an isolated instance; numerous biblical accounts share a similar commitment to truthfulness, revealing the strengths and weaknesses of even the most revered figures.

This raises a compelling question: why don't spiritual organizations, like the church, follow the biblical example of transparency and honesty? Why do they often shy away from acknowledging their own flaws, mistakes, and shortcomings? By emulating the Bible's approach, churches can foster a culture of authenticity, accountability, and trust, allowing them to more effectively serve their congregations and communities.

This phenomenon of selective historical representation is not unique to the church in Zimbabwe; the mother church in South Africa has also been guilty of adopting a "history is written by the victors" mindset. Despite having extensive records in their archives, the church's portrayal of Thomas Hezmalhalch, for example, is incomplete and biased. This lack of transparency and accuracy in historical representation is a recurring issue, perpetuating a narrative that favors the dominant voices while marginalizing others.

A significant controversy surrounds the legacy of Thomas Hezmalhalch within the Apostolic Faith Mission (AFM). Many members of the church downplay his contributions, attributing his election as the first president of the AFM to his seniority rather than his leadership abilities. They suggest that Hezmalhalch's age may have been the deciding factor in his selection, implying that he may not have been the most qualified candidate for the position. Some even speculate that John Lake, a prominent figure in the early Pentecostal movement, would have been the preferred choice for the presidency if not for Hezmalhalch's advanced age.

This perspective overlooks Hezmalhalch's significant role in the formative years of the AFM, including his involvement in the Azusa Street Revival and his missionary work in South Africa. By diminishing his achievements, members may be inadvertently perpetuating a narrative that neglects the complex dynamics and personalities that shaped the church's early history. A more nuanced understanding of Hezmalhalch's presidency and contributions could provide valuable insights into the AFM's development and the challenges it faced during its formative years.

Before embarking on their African mission, Thomas Hezmalhalch, a preacher from the American Holiness Church, and John Lake, a former elder of the Zion City Apostolic Church, collaborated on a successful gospel campaign in Zion City, Illinois. This partnership laid the groundwork for their future endeavors. In a remarkable display of devotion, both Lake and Hezmalhalch sold all their possessions before departing for South Africa. Their bold decision was motivated by a desire to become "wholly dependent upon God" for their support, abandoning themselves entirely to the preaching of Jesus.

This remarkable act of surrender and trust in God's provision parallels the story of Elisha, a prophet in the Old Testament. When Elisha was called by God through Elijah, he dramatically demonstrated his commitment to following God's will by destroying all his bridges to his former life (1 Kings 19:19-21). He slaughtered his span of oxen, which represented his livelihood and source of income, and burned the wooden plows, rendering them useless. By doing so, Elisha eliminated any possibility of returning to his old life if the going got tough. He was, in essence, declaring, "I have no other recourse but to depend solely on God."

Similarly, Lake and Hezmalhalch's decision to sell all their possessions and rely on God's provision demonstrated a profound trust in His sovereignty and faithfulness. By severing their ties to material security, they were able to focus on their mission and ministry, unencumbered by the burdens of personal resources.

Following his one-year term as the first president of the Apostolic Faith Mission (AFM), Thomas Hezmalhalch returned to the United States, paving the way for John G. Lake to assume the presidency. Lake led the church from 1909 until 1913, when he also departed for the USA, leaving a void in leadership.

On November 11, 1913, Rev. Le Roux was elected as the third president of the AFM, marking the beginning of a remarkable 30-year tenure. Under his leadership, the church experienced significant growth and development, with Rev. Le Roux playing a crucial role in shaping the AFM's doctrine and practices. However, due to deteriorating health, Rev. Le Roux relinquished his position in 1943.

Rev. F.P. Moller succeeded Rev. Le Roux, becoming the fourth president of the AFM in 1943. Rev. Moller's presidency spanned 22 years, until 1965. During his tenure, the church continued to expand its reach and influence, with Rev. Moller building on the foundations laid by his predecessors.

It's noteworthy that John Graham Lake's initial experience of receiving the Holy Spirit and speaking in tongues occurred when he accompanied Thomas Hezmalhalch to pray for a sick lady, at Hezmalhalch's invitation. This significant event highlights the equal partnership and collaborative spirit between Lake and Hezmalhalch in their service to the Lord. However, it's striking that Lake often receives more recognition and celebration than Hezmalhalch, which reflects a natural yet worldly tendency to elevate certain individuals over others.

This phenomenon is reminiscent of the biblical account of Elijah, who thought he was the only remaining prophet of God, only to be corrected by the Lord, who revealed that there were 400 other prophets still faithful (1 Kings 19:18). This story serves as a poignant reminder that the value we assign to God's servants is not always aligned with God's own assessment. Similarly, in the New Testament, Jesus' disciples attempted to rebuke a man who was casting out demons in Jesus' name, simply because he wasn't part of their inner circle (Mark 9:38-40). Jesus, however, gently rebuked their narrow-mindedness, emphasizing that anyone working in His name was an ally, regardless of their affiliation.

It's also worth noting that Thomas Hezmalhalch was older than Lake, but their partnership was built on mutual respect and merit, rather than age or politics. Hezmalhalch's contributions to their shared ministry were invaluable, and his legacy deserves equal recognition and celebration.

Indeed, it's evident that God occasionally orchestrates conflicts or tensions within united groups to achieve a greater purpose. A prime example is the Tower of Babel, where God, although impressed by humanity's unity and capabilities, confused their languages to redirect them towards His original plan of dispersing them across the earth (Genesis 11:1-9). Similarly, in the early Christian church, God allowed persecution in Jerusalem, prompting the Apostles to scatter and fulfill their commission to spread the Gospel globally, making disciples for Christ (Acts 8:1-4).

Another instance is the replacement of Judas Iscariot, where God seemingly overlooked the selection of Matthias and instead chose Saul of Tarsus (Paul) for a more significant role in spreading Christianity (Acts 9:1-31). In this context, it's possible that God allowed tension between Lake and Hezmalhalch to propel Lake into a more prominent role, aligning with His sovereign plan.

However, it's crucial for historians to present these events accurately, without bias or embellishment, acknowledging the complexities and nuances of God's workings. By doing so, we can gain a deeper understanding of God's providence and the ways in which He shapes human events to achieve His purposes.

A crucial aspect of the Apostolic Faith Mission's (AFM) history, often overlooked, is the church's origins in the United States. Founded in 1906 by William Joseph Seymour, a key figure in the early Pentecostal movement, the AFM's roots are deeply embedded in American soil. Seymour's ministry in Los Angeles, particularly at the Azusa Street Revival, significantly shaped the AFM's doctrine and practices. The Apostolic Faith Mission of South Africa, established in 1908, was an extension of Seymour's original church, making it the South African chapter of the global AFM movement.

This historical connection highlights the transnational nature of the early Pentecostal movement, which spread rapidly across the globe, crossing cultural and geographical boundaries. The AFM's growth in South Africa was influenced by the missionary work of early Pentecostal pioneers, who carried Seymour's teachings and vision to African shores. Understanding the AFM's

American roots provides valuable context for appreciating its development, challenges, and contributions to the religious landscape of South Africa.

Notably, the South African chapter of the AFM was autonomous and independent from the control of the Los Angeles church. Despite this, the church in South Africa maintained a level of control over the Zimbabwean chapter, which raises questions about the motivations behind this decision.

Furthermore, it is essential to acknowledge the true founders of the Church in Zimbabwe, who were the migrant workers of Matabeleland South in December 1908, including Lukas Mutokwa. Their contributions to the establishment and growth of the church in Zimbabwe are often overlooked, and their legacy deserves recognition.

CHAPTER ten

Breakaways and Schisms: Understanding the Complexities of Church Division

Breakaways in Christian churches can occur for a variety of complex and interconnected reasons. Disagreements over doctrine and theology can lead to divisions, as members may hold differing interpretations of scripture or theological beliefs. Leadership conflicts, including power struggles, disagreements over leadership style, or concerns about a leader's integrity, can also cause breakaways.

Furthermore, differences in opinion on church governance, decision-making processes, or organizational structure can lead to divisions. Additionally, conflicts over worship styles, liturgy, or practices can cause some members to leave and form new churches.

Personal conflicts and relationships can also play a role, as unresolved issues, hurt feelings, or strained relationships between members or leaders can lead to breakaways. Cultural and ethnic differences within churches can also lead to divisions, as diverse values, customs, or communication styles may clash.

Disagreements over the church's vision, mission, or direction can also cause breakaways, as members may have differing ideas about the church's purpose or future. In some cases, allegations of abuse, mismanagement, or corruption can lead to breakaways as members lose trust in leadership.

Denominational affiliation can also be a point of contention, with disagreements over affiliation changes or a desire for independence leading to breakaways. Finally, personal ambition can sometimes drive individuals to break away and start their own churches, seeking control or a sense of fulfillment.

Reporting breakaways truthfully and the repercussions thereof helps the church to confront its flaws, acknowledge the role of human error, and learn from past experiences. By examining the complexities of church politics, leadership struggles, and the impact of external factors, the AFM in Zimbabwe can gain valuable insights into its own growth, identity, and mission. This honest reflection enables the church to refine its approach, foster greater unity, and move forward with a renewed commitment to its core values and purpose.

The first recorded breakaway from the Apostolic Faith Mission (AFM) occurred in 1907 in America, before the church's expansion to Africa. Florence Crawford, Seymour's State Director of the Pacific Coast Apostolic Faith Movement, broke away to form the Apostolic Faith (movement) Church of Oregon, with the assistance of Clara Lum, the editor of the Apostolic Faith publication. This schism was fueled by Seymour's plans to launch the broader Apostolic Faith Movement, a name previously used by Charles Parham, who attempted to claim leadership of the Azusa Street Revival.

The situation was further complicated by Seymour's marriage to Jennie Evans Moore on May 13, 1908, which led to Clara Lum's resignation and her subsequent theft of the mailing list. Lum joined Crawford in Portland, and together they began publishing The Apostolic Faith newspaper without Seymour's consent. Despite Seymour's demands, Lum and Crawford refused to return control of the paper, dealing a significant blow to the Azusa revival.

This incident raises questions about the motivations and actions of those involved, who claimed to be doing God's work while engaging in deceitful behavior. However, as the Bible attests, God remains faithful, and the breakaway church continues to operate to this day. Jesus' words in Matthew 7:22-23 come to mind, where He says that some will claim to have done mighty works in His name, only to be told to depart from Him. The church's prosperity is not dependent on its leaders' flaws, as God's plans cannot be thwarted by human error, just as He spared the city of Nineveh despite Jonah's disobedience.

In 1960, fifty-three years after the initial breakaway in the United States, Morgan Sengwayo, a former deacon and teacher in Lower Gwelo, Zimbabwe, broke away from the Zimbabwean chapter of the Apostolic Faith Mission of South Africa to form the Apostolic Faith Mission of Africa. Notably, Sengwayo affiliated his new church with Florence Crawford's Apostolic Faith Church of Oregon, which had been established in 1907 after Crawford's breakaway from William Joseph Seymour's Apostolic Faith Mission.

This affiliation highlights the transnational connections and shared histories between early Pentecostal movements. Sengwayo's decision to align with Crawford's church, rather than remaining with the South African chapter, suggests a desire for autonomy and a distinctive theological or doctrinal emphasis. The Apostolic Faith Mission of Africa, under Sengwayo's leadership, would go on to develop its own unique character and contribute to the diverse landscape of Pentecostalism in Africa.

The Apostolic Faith Mission (AFM) has experienced numerous breakaways throughout its history, leading to the formation of various churches. One such breakaway occurred in 2019 when Edward Lion, a former member of the AFM, left to form the Zion Apostolic Faith Mission. Notably, Lion had previously been a member of Zion Christianity before joining the AFM. Another notable breakaway is attributed to Engenas Lekganyane, who is claimed by some to have been a member of the Zion Apostolic Faith Mission, while others assert that he was part of the Apostolic Faith Mission of South Africa. Regardless, both the ZAFM and Lekganyane's Zion Christian Church (ZCC) have their roots in the AFM of South Africa.

Samuel Moyo, also known as Samuel Mutendi, is another example of a breakaway leader. AFM records indicate that he broke away from the church, while others claim that he left Engenas Lekganyane's ZCC. Nonetheless, Moyo's connection to the AFM is undeniable, whether as a son or grandson.

This modern Zionist movement, which blends elements of church and cult, combines spiritual healing with African traditional practices. By synchronizing Christianity with African Traditional Religion beliefs and practices, including polygamy, they create a unique syncretic approach. For healing and curing, they utilize everyday items like water, milk, eggs, honey, tea, or coffee, which they bless with prayer sayings. Additionally, they incorporate garments, robes, and cloths of various colors into their rituals, similar to African Traditional Religion healers.

This blending of Christianity with African culture attracts many followers who feel a sense of familiarity and comfort in combining their faith with traditional practices. However, this approach raises concerns among conservative Christians who question the legitimacy and morality of these practices. While some elements may be familiar in religious contexts, they are often taken to extremes, making it challenging to distinguish between what is considered godly and what may be deemed evil.

Other notable breakaways include Matthew Chigagazvimba and Mai Chaza (1924), whose biographies do not mention any links to the AFM, despite being listed as former members in AFM records. Similarly, Shonhihwa Masedza (also known as Johane Masowe) of 1934 is mentioned in AFM records as a former member, but his biography does not acknowledge this connection. Isaac Chiumbu of the 1943 split is mentioned in AFM records as a former member, and his own records acknowledge it.

Ezekiel Handinawangu Guti, who broke away in the late 1950s, also appears to distance himself from the AFM in his writings. Additionally, Elijah Mugodhi (1945-1948 split) and Madida Moyo (1945), who founded the Pure Apostolic Faith Mission, are among those who broke away from the AFM.

It is evident that many of these breakaways have been marked by disputed histories, with both sides often presenting biased accounts. This lack of honesty makes it challenging to assign blame or credit to one party over the other.

In the midst of breakaways and divisions, a common phenomenon emerges: no faction admits fault or wrongdoing. Instead, each side points accusatory fingers at the other, engaging in a blame game that obscures the truth. This lack of accountability and humility is contrary to the biblical principle outlined in Philippians 2:3, which exhorts believers to "Let nothing be done through strife or vainglory; but in lowliness of mind let each esteem other better than themselves."

This passage emphasizes the importance of humility, selflessness, and mutual respect in resolving conflicts and building strong relationships. By esteeming others better than ourselves, we acknowledge their value and worth, creating an environment conducive to constructive dialogue and reconciliation.

In the context of church breakaways, this means that both sides should engage in introspection, acknowledging their own contributions to the conflict and seeking forgiveness where necessary. By doing so, they can work towards healing, restoration, and potentially even reunification.

Unfortunately, the absence of this humility and willingness to listen often perpetuates cycles of strife and division, hindering the church's witness and effectiveness in sharing the Gospel. As believers, it's essential to remember that our unity and love for one another are paramount, reflecting the very nature of God Himself (John 17:20-23).

The case of Elijah Mugodhi (1899-1971), founder of the Apostolic Faith Church, presents an intriguing example of conflicting narratives. Mugodhi was installed as bishop of the Apostolic Faith Church at Chitsunge, Chokore Village in Buhera in 1948. However, the circumstances surrounding his installation are shrouded in controversy, with different versions of the story emerging.

According to a reliable source, Mugodhi's wife experienced a mysterious and prolonged menstrual period lasting thirteen years. His in-laws, in an attempt to compensate him, offered the younger sister as a second wife. Mugodhi accepted, but this decision was met with disapproval from the head office in Johannesburg. A delegation was sent to Hwedza to investigate and try Mugodhi's case, along with local elders, over several months. The deliberations reached a deadlock, with two main points of contention. Mugodhi and his congregation believed that the missionaries should pray for the healing of his wife before he could send away the second wife. In contrast, the disciplinary panel maintained that the church did not condone polygamy, citing regulations that encouraged polygamous men to retain only their senior wife.

The standoff continued until 1948, when a remarkable event occurred during the proceedings. A tree with a Y-shape at Mugodhi's home suddenly broke into two, with each side falling in opposite directions. A white missionary from South Africa interpreted this phenomenon as a sign that the church had split into two, with no provision for reunification. This event was taken as a divine signal, leading to the parting of ways between Mugodhi and the Apostolic Faith Mission.

However, a parallel narrative suggests that Mugodhi married the second wife due to his first wife's blindness. This account is disputed as a misinterpretation of a wise explanation. The elders in the village understood the phrase "the wife had become blind" as a proverbial expression meaning the couple had lost hope for intimacy, rather than literal blindness.

The conflicting accounts surrounding Mugodhi's case highlight the complexities and nuances of church history, where different perspectives and interpretations can lead to varying narratives.

In terms of doctrine, the Apostolic Faith Mission (AFM) and the Apostolic Faith Church (AFC) founded by Elijah Mugodhi share a significant amount of common ground. While there may be some minor variations, the core beliefs and principles of the two churches are largely aligned.

One area where the AFC differs slightly from the AFM is in its approach to polygamy. The original church founded by Mugodhi does not promote or encourage polygamy as a general practice. However, it does provide for exceptional cases, such as the one Mugodhi himself faced, where a second marriage may be permitted under specific circumstances.

Unfortunately, this provision has been exploited by some individuals who have taken advantage of the flexibility to justify their own desires for multiple marriages. This has led to numerous breakaways and the formation of splinter groups, which have deviated from the original teachings and principles of the AFC.

These breakaways have not only caused division within the church but have also tarnished the reputation of the AFC and its founder, Elijah Mugodhi. Despite these challenges, the AFC remains committed to its core values and continues to uphold the principles of its founder, while also acknowledging the need for wisdom and discernment in addressing complex issues like polygamy.

While it is true that the official recognition of the Apostolic Faith Mission (AFM) in 1947 brought about a semblance of order and discipline, it is misleading to suggest that this led to the voluntary or forced departure of those who disagreed with the church's stance. Biased accounts often highlight the expulsion of black leaders for alleged misconduct, such as adultery or polygamy, without acknowledging the church's own flaws and shortcomings.

The truth is that the church was complicit in racial segregation, mirroring the discriminatory practices of the government at the time. While many choose to gloss over this uncomfortable fact, they continue to blame those who broke away from the church. Unfortunately, most black members rely on accounts from their colonial masters, lacking access to balanced records of events. Notably, there is no evidence of white missionaries being held accountable for their actions, despite opposition from whites in America and South Africa against John Lake and the AFM.

The Wikipedia page on John Lake, edited primarily by non-Africans, presents a narrative that may be perceived as skewed or inaccurate by Zimbabwean congregants of the Apostolic Faith Mission (AFM). However, it is ironic that these same congregants often perpetuate a biased view of black leaders who challenged the church's and government's segregational laws, labeling them as outcasts simply because the missionaries deemed them guilty. This highlights a concerning dynamic where African voices and perspectives are often marginalized or dismissed, even within their own communities. It is essential to acknowledge and address these biases, ensuring that the stories and contributions of black leaders are accurately represented and celebrated. By doing so, we can work towards a more inclusive and nuanced understanding of history.

In reality, these schisms and expulsions led to the formation of numerous apostolic churches, a fact acknowledged by at least one Zimbabwean black author. A more nuanced understanding of this complex history is essential to confront the church's past and promote healing and unity.

Zimbabwean congregants of the Apostolic Faith Mission (AFM) have a complex and problematic relationship with the church's history of racial segregation. Notably, they do not express concern over the "whites-only" church that operated in Zimbabwe during the colonial era, which actively supported and perpetuated racial segregation. This is evident in the fact that white members of the AFM in Zimbabwe abruptly left the church en masse in

1983, when the local leadership transitioned to black leaders. This exodus was not a result of expulsion, but rather a refusal to submit to black leadership.

Today, the AFM in Zimbabwe has no white members nationwide, a stark testament to the deep-seated racial tensions and biases that persist within the church. Despite this, many AFM members continue to trust and accept the narratives and accounts provided by their former white leaders, even when these accounts are critical or dismissive of pioneering black leaders like Isaac Chiumbu, Shonhihwa Masedza, Morgan Sengwayo, Madida Moyo, Ezekiel Handinawangu Guti, and Elijah Mugodhi.

This phenomenon raises important questions about the ongoing legacy of colonialism and racism within the AFM in Zimbabwe, and the need for a critical re-examination of the church's history and leadership dynamics. By confronting and addressing these issues, the AFM in Zimbabwe can work towards a more inclusive and equitable future, one that honors the contributions and experiences of all its members, regardless of race or political affiliation.

It is essential to recognize that a leader's flaws and shortcomings may impact the visible church, but they cannot destroy the invisible church that operates within it. The invisible church, comprised of true believers and followers of Christ, remains unaffected by the flaws of human leadership.

This is evident in the numerous churches that have broken away from the Apostolic Faith Mission (AFM), either directly or indirectly. Despite the challenges and controversies surrounding their separation, these churches are thriving and experiencing numerical growth. While numerical growth is a visible indicator of success, it is essential to acknowledge that spiritual growth is a more critical measure of a church's health.

All denominations, including those that have broken away from AFM, have an invisible church within them. This invisible church is comprised of individuals who are genuinely committed to their faith and are striving to live according to God's will. However, it is also possible that some prominent elements within the visible church may be found unworthy on the day of judgment.

The church that Jesus Christ founded is not dependent on human leadership or institutions. It is a spiritual entity that transcends the flaws and failures of its human representatives. As the Bible says, "the gates of Hades will not prevail against it" (Matthew 16:18). Even if the visible church leadership falls, there will always be those who remain faithful and committed to the end.

This is a testament to the enduring power of the invisible church, which is not bound by human limitations or flaws. As the apostle Paul wrote, "the Lord knows those who are his" (2 Timothy 2:19), and it is this invisible church that will ultimately stand the test of time and judgment.

While the Apostolic Faith Mission (AFM) is undeniably the mother of Pentecostalism in Africa, its legacy is marred by a tumultuous history of breakaways and schisms. Despite its significant contributions to the growth of Pentecostalism on the continent, the AFM has struggled to reproduce church denominations in a peaceful and orderly manner. This has resulted in numerous splinter groups and breakaway churches, often formed by charismatic leaders who felt stifled or marginalized within the AFM.

It is crucial for the AFM to recognize the value of empowering younger pastors and individuals with potential to form their own ministries or church denominations. By blessing and releasing them to pursue their calling, the AFM can foster a culture of multiplication and growth, rather than trying to control or dominate the spread of Pentecostalism.

The AFM's inability to let go and allow new leaders to emerge may be attributed to a "Tower of Babel mentality," where the focus is on building a centralized, monolithic institution rather than scattering and spreading the Gospel. However, as the Bible reminds us, God is always in control, and His plans cannot be thwarted by human ambition or pride. The breakaways and schisms may, in fact, be a divine catalyst for the spread of Pentecostalism, as new leaders and churches emerge to fulfill God's purposes.

By embracing a spirit of humility, multiplication, and release, the AFM can rediscover its role as a mother church, nurturing and empowering new generations of leaders to carry the torch of Pentecostalism forward.

When church denominations and ministries are reproduced in a peaceful and orderly manner, they can maintain a healthy connection with their parent church, in this case, the Apostolic Faith Mission (AFM). This allows for a sense of continuity and shared heritage, rather than the current situation where breakaway denominations often attempt to sever ties and conceal their historical links with AFM.

Ironically, these breakaway groups try to hide their past associations with AFM, but this deception is only effective in the eyes of humans. God, being all-knowing, is fully aware of their journey and the attempts to distort their history. By denying their roots, these groups demonstrate hypocrisy and dishonesty, which can hinder their relationship with God.

It's worth noting that acknowledging one's spiritual heritage is essential for growth and accountability. Just as a person proudly acknowledges their educational background, from kindergarten to PhD, churches should also embrace their spiritual lineage. By doing so, they can build on the foundations laid by their predecessors and continue to grow and learn.

In contrast, attempting to erase or conceal one's spiritual history can lead to a loss of identity and authenticity. It's essential for churches to embrace their past, learn from it, and use it as a stepping stone for future growth, rather than trying to hide or distort it. By doing so, they can maintain a clear conscience before God and humanity.

In conclusion, I often wonder what would have been if my grandfather, Jenias Mufambi Chikwinya, and my father, Katazo Amos Magundwane, had received formal education. Perhaps they could have played a more prominent role in shaping the history of the Apostolic Faith Mission of South Africa, the Zimbabwe chapter. Unfortunately, they were denied this opportunity due to the societal constraints of their time.

My mother, Resiya Magundwane (née Chikwinya), and her brother, Naphtali Mufambi Chikwinya, were fortunate enough to receive some formal education, albeit only up to mid-primary school level. This limited education was not considered sufficient to be deemed "educated" in the eyes of the church and society.

Despite the lack of formal education, both my maternal grandfather and father were self-taught and possessed remarkable skills. They could read and write in four languages, three of which they spoke fluently. However, this was not enough to secure them admission to Bible school, a requirement for leadership positions within the AFM.

In crafting this narrative, I drew upon the collective knowledge and experiences shared by my mother and uncle, which were passed down to them from their father, my maternal grandfather, Jenias Mufambi Chikwinya. Their contributions have provided invaluable insights into the history of the AFM in Zimbabwe, particularly regarding the church's development within the country.

While I did not directly quote their statements or attribute specific comments to individuals, I have woven their accounts into my own narrative, supported by my own research and verification. My family's knowledge primarily concerns the church's development within Zimbabwe, while their understanding of the church's history outside the country is based on information shared by missionaries and migrant workers. I have supplemented this with my own research to provide a comprehensive narrative.

The accounts presented in this narrative are verifiable through various sources, including the Apostolic Faith Mission of South Africa archives in Johannesburg, the National Archives in Zimbabwe, and works of other authors, both online and in books. I deliberately chose not to cite specific sources, as most of my contributions are based on oral narratives from my family members. However, I have verified all information to ensure accuracy and authenticity.

And so, I have a deep affection for the Apostolic Faith Mission (AFM) church, rooted in my family's history and legacy in Zimbabwe. The church has been my source of solace, guidance, and community, shaping me through its teachings and values. I've witnessed its impact on countless lives and am grateful for its presence in mine. Despite challenges and controversies, my commitment remains unwavering. I believe in redemption, forgiveness, and growth, and I'm excited to see the AFM evolve and adapt to changing needs. A more nuanced understanding of the church's complex history is essential to confront the past and promote healing and unity. I am proud to be a part of this community and will continue to serve, support, and love the AFM with all my heart, as long as it continues to profess that the Lord, Jesus Christ, is its head.

ABOUT THE AUTHOR

Jaison Ndlovu, born on July 1, 1960, in Guruve, Zimbabwe, grew up in Bharamasvesve, Zhombe, Kwekwe. He is the second child and eldest son of Katazo Amos Magundwane and Resiya Chikwinya. With four sisters and four brothers, he attended Gwesela St Andrew's School, St Martin de Porres, and Ascot Secondary School for his education. He pursued salesmanship at the Union College of South Africa and Religious Studies at Ambassador Bible College. Jaison is married to Susan Ndlovu (nee Mahogo), and they have four sons and two daughters, all of whom are married. Staying at Empress in Zhombe, Zimbabwe, he is an active contributor as a blogger and editor on Wikipedia, and shares video songs and sermons on YouTube.